The Problems

With

Religion

The Problems with Religion

Jim E. Barrett, Ed.D

The Problems With Religion
Jim E. Barrett.

Includes bibliographical references and index

For my father Hap the Carpenter,
who taught me to question everything,
to work hard and play hard,
to like myself and to love life.
He said
*"Son if you want to get close
to your maker, go out in the woods and
sit very quietly on an old cedar stump."*

Acknowledgements

Thanks to my family for their encouragement and understanding. Their love means everything to me. Thanks to my long time friend and professional colleague, Bill Harrison, for all his encouragement, counsel, and wonderful editing assistance. Thanks to my son, Brian, for his assistance on the cover. Thanks to my evangelical minister nephew, Paul Barrett, for not killing me as scripture instructs, answering all my questions, and providing his point of view.

Thanks to all those free thinkers and rational people who have dared to question, had the wisdom to think for themselves, and had the courage to publish, so that we can make this world a better place, without hatred and violence.

Contents

Part 4 -- Some Possible Solutions

"The afterlife-obsessed suicidal brain really is a weapon of immense power and danger. It is comparable to a smart missile.. yet . . . it is very, very cheap . . . To fill a world with religion, or religions of the Abrahamic kind, is like littering the streets with loaded guns. Do not be surprised if they use them.."

Richard Dawkins

Part 1 - - Introduction And Overview

Introduction

When I started this project of inquiry about religion, I had no intention of writing a book. I do not consider myself a professional author. I'm a husband, a father, a part-time boat captain, a retired university educator, and a concerned American wanting the best life possible for my children and grandchildren. As a young person, I was fascinated by anthropology, social evolution and cultural diversity, but life and the need to make a living got in the way of my fascination, and, until retirement, there never seemed to be time available to spend on such subjects.

I have traveled widely, enjoyed many cultures, and developed friendships around the world. I felt reasonably content with my understanding of human diversity and social awareness, but there is one area that was especially confusing, and that is religion. So a few years ago I began a research project to seek answers to some questions I had about religion:

- Why is religion so prevalent?

- Where does religion come from?

- Why is religion so important to believers?

- Why don't people talk about religion?

These basic questions led to others, and now that I have several bookcases full of books about religion, as well as books on human history, evolution, physics and philosophy, I have decided to write down what I have learned. In addition, I have added what I now consider the "Big Problems" with religion and some suggestions, some possible answers as to how we might solve them.

These are my personal conclusions; I do not claim that any one of them is unquestionably correct, or even the only answer. They are just what I have concluded from my studies. The topic of religion is one of considerable disagreement; even the historical accounting of religious events is often challenged, and the authors of many religious works are unknown. What I have tried to do is to be respectful of all beliefs, use reason, and stay focused on what changes and outcomes could lead all people toward a more positive future. The bibliography includes most of the works that have helped me come to my conclusions.

I recently read all the way through many of the primary holy books, including the Bible. I had tried to read the Bible many times, but I always got bored and could not find much that was helpful or engaging except from a historical perspective. Overall, the Bible is devilishly difficult to read as a logical book because it is more of a collection of disjointed books. The King James Version, for example, was translated into 1700's era Old English and is exceedingly hard to understand. In addition, much of it is written as poetry or verse, such as the book of Proverbs, with other portions being accounts of wars between desert tribes. In addition, there are many detailed listings of family genealogy and descriptions of life in the desert approximately 1600 years ago.

I have learned that many self-identified believers have not read much of their basic religious texts. If you are a believer of one of the major world wide religions, I urge you to do some careful study. I especially recommend the Torah (first five books of the Bible – Jewish scripture) to believers of the Jewish faith and the entire Bible to believers of the Christian faiths. A 2010 Pew Research Report on religious knowledge surveyed 3,412 Americans and found that the average person could only correctly answer 16 out of 32 basic knowledge questions on religion. Those identifying themselves as atheist or agnostic scored the highest with 20.9 correctly-answered questions. Mainstream protestants averaged only 15.8 correctly-answered questions. It seems only appropriate that, if a person identifies with a faith, they should at least read their holy books to understand what they actually say.

I also read all the way through the Book of Mormon. It has a relatively modern introduction, but it then goes into stories retold from the Bible, written by a family leaving Jerusalem and wandering around in the desert in approximately the year 500. They document many descendants, tell of running into a number of other tribes, get involved in wars, and record the death of kings and the daily activities of many tribal leaders. Overall, the book describes how desperate and difficult life was 1500 years ago in the middle-east, where violence, theft, slavery, and murder were a prominent part of everyday life.

The Qur'an (the primary holy book of the Islamic faith) was a surprise to me, as I expected to read statements of gender abuse, discrimination, and encouragement of violence. While it is true that these statements are in the Qur'an, they were far less prevalent than I had expected. In fact, it is rather peaceful overall, with considerable references to the idea of being kind and generous to fellow believers in Allah. The constant repetition within the book seems intended to be hypnotic, where readers are constantly reminded that everything is about their god, with "In the name of Allah, the Beneficent, the Merciful" repeated over and over. However, the many hadiths (words and deeds of the prophet Mohammed), which are also considered sacred writings, contain much suggested abuse and violence, and the clerics of Islam are prone to teach such violence as religious law. So do not misunderstand me -- Islam is terribly scary.

After reading the books listed in the appendix, I started writing about my findings related to my original questions listed above. It soon became abundantly clear that there are some enormous problems related to the major religions, and for the most part, they are not being discussed openly. These significant problems are not talked about, they are almost never mentioned in the press, nor are they even likely to be found in published material.

For the most part, there is a universal desire to be exceedingly polite when mentioning anyone's religion or when commenting on the holy books that the faithful believe to be the word of god. Many believe these books to be divinely written, or at least checked over by their god to make sure they are entirely true and accurate. In reality, most of these sacred books are thousands of years old, were written hundreds of years after the events they describe, have been translated many times, and have been extensively edited -- all by mere mortals. How the believers of these faiths interpret their holy books and use them to guide their feelings, their thoughts, and their actions relating to other people, are the "big problems" focused on in this book.

Nothing inherently makes the world's religions and their scriptures out of bounds for discussion and intellectual challenge. As educated people, we need to understand what the major religions of the world are teaching and what they encourage their followers to think and do. These religions literally affect all of our lives every day. It is time everyone realizes that, while religion is important, we must recognize how religious fundamentalism reduces our chance for world peace, encourages abuse of women and children, impedes knowledge, and, most importantly, could very possibly destroy humanity on this planet. Above all else, we must understand how the holy books and those who promote their literal teachings, poison the minds of believers, and cause death and destruction world-wide.

Pointing out these problems is not my only goal. I am intending to encourage remedial action; we can all make a difference in a positive direction. We can start talking and learning about the religions of the world and how each religion affects its followers and the decisions they make. Most importantly, we can start a change that will reduce hatred, promote humane treatment for all people, and make this a safer and better world for our children and grandchildren.

From my study on this issue, I have increased my appreciation for the complexity of religion and for the good it can provide. I now have a better understanding of those who believe in a god or gods, and I have increased my tolerance and respect for those practicing a belief system.

My work here is not about bashing anyone or wanting to take away anyone's faith in a god. Having a belief in a supernatural god is not the problem; the problem is when the scriptures endorsed by that god, as interpreted by their followers, encourage inhumane behavior towards other people.

I find it necessary to define several terms used in discussing religion. While our English language is full of religious words, the meanings of these words are not always clear or commonly shared by everyone. In my research, I would often have to stop and look up a word, only to find that there were several ways the word could be used, depending on which religion was using it. I will be as brief as possible in my definitions, but I do want you to know what I mean by each label or term.

What is Religion?

What is a religion? I thought it would be easy to define religion. Instead, I have found it very hard because there are so many types and varieties of beliefs that people call religion, and they often have little in common. But just so we are on the same general topic, here is my best shot: Religion is a belief system which involves the supernatural and, usually, has something to do with what happens after death.

Not all supernatural beliefs are religions. People believe in Big Foot, the Locke Ness Monster, and space aliens but they do not call these religious beliefs. Yet some beliefs in aliens are religions with the hope of an alien-supported afterlife, so it gets mighty complicated to sort out which supernatural beliefs are the foundation of a religion and which are merely supernatural beliefs. Some beliefs such as "luck," special numbers, and all kinds of other spiritual concepts don't seem like religions, but the extent to which people sometimes pray for or about these things, thinking such prayer will change their lives, do make even these seem like religions.

I have given up on a single, comprehensive definition of the word religion. I moved on to investigate the question, what is the essence of experiencing religious beliefs. Specifically, I mean a belief in a god or gods, in demons, ghosts, reincarnation, spirits and in a supernatural afterlife that does not require a physical body.

Many social anthropologists, cognitive psychologists, and biological researchers now believe this thing we call religion is a normal by-product or side-effect of the evolutionary development of the human mind. That is, as the human brain developed over time there evolved concepts of perception, emotion, and social structure, as well as other similar concepts, which gradually developed and became interrelated. As the complexity of the human mind developed over millions of years, the interrelationship of these concepts came to allow modern humans to perceive distinct thoughts, and one of these thoughts or concepts is what we call religion.

For example, we developed the unique ability to understand our own mortality, which normally plays a vital part in religion. We also have developed the ability to make assumptions about others' motives, and we have learned that what people say is not always what they mean. This ability to recognize and perform deception, and to presume intent in what others are likely thinking and feeling, is a key part of human experience that is understood and expressed in what we call religion. Religion provides the ability to believe without evidence, to come up with answers to things we do not or cannot understand, and to apply human-like personality traits to superhuman agents. In short, most scientists say religion is possible as a mental construct because of our unique human mind and that it is a by-product of the interrelationship of other useful mental concepts.

Let me explain a little more about how the human mind uniquely can and does support the capacity for the concept of religion. First, each of the cognitive concepts I mentioned has some adaptive quality that has allowed humans as a species to survive and continue to evolve. For example, understanding that another group may be acting in a friendly way, yet may be secretly planning to do violence, has likely saved many people from an early death and allowed them to reproduce. Scientists generally agree that, while religion or belief in the supernatural itself does not seem to have a direct adaptive advantage for keeping humans alive, it is these other mental developments or modules, such as the ability to perceive deception and the fear of humans that were different, that did have survival advantages. They combined with each other and eventually allowed religion as a construct to develop and, over time, to be retained in future generations. Thus, religion might be called a "by product." It was likely not needed as a fundamental survival skill, but it developed from the interrelationships of concepts that did provide a survival advantage.

On the other hand, some evolutionary biologists believe that supernatural beliefs or religion may have had a more direct survival factor in making primitive man more cautious, and therefore religion developed as a personal safety feature that kept early humanoids alive. For example, early humans who feared a demon of the night might have survived better than groups who got eaten by nocturnal predators.

Regardless of all the complicated psychological theories on how religion came to exist in the human mind, it is clear that whatever it is and however it developed, it has been with us for many thousands of years, likely as long as language itself, and we have obviously evolved, as humans, with the ability to believe in supernatural phenomenon. In fact, most social biologists believe that this thing we call religion is now mostly genetic, and we automatically have a tendency to believe in supernatural agents.

Dr. Robert Buckman, a Canadian physician, writes about how religion is located in our limbic system and, more specifically, in the right-sided temporal lobe. He cites numerous studies that demonstrate that when an electrical stimulation of this area of the brain is induced, the subject will feel themselves in the presence of a god, have out-of-body experiences, and even hear the "voice of god." Like all physical sensitivities, some people are more prone to this feeling than others and may experience these feelings with extremely little external stimulation, or even sometimes with none. He says, *"It has been demonstrated, unequivocally and unambiguously, the experience of God is built into the human mind. The God of mind is undeniable."* It seems we are hardwired to be able to feel spiritual about many things.

Early humans were likely ancestor worshipers, believing that the dead talked to them and had control over their lives. Later, they gave spiritual "power" to all kinds of things -- animals, trees, mountains, and even the solar system (animism) -- that they believed controlled their lives and provided answers to things they could not otherwise understand. This was the way for many thousands of years that literally hundreds of thousands of generations of people believed in spirits, demons and ghosts; in fact, many still do.

People believe in all kinds of supernatural things that they fold into religion. On the one hand are the fully formed gods with omnipotent powers, such as in Christianity and Hinduism, and on the other are the animistic beliefs of spirits and even things like karma, space travelers, witches, demons and ghosts. Almost all of these beliefs involve human-like qualities and yet are differentiated from humans, making them supernatural. It is difficult to see where a lucky number starts and a full blown belief in a god or gods stop. All of these beliefs are forms of religion.

Personalities are often given to spirits. For example, one of the Native American religions has animal spirits that are tricksters, such as the raven, or wise and helpful spirits who can give advice and are located on mountain tops or special "holy" places. Many people, especially in Asia, believe in the spiritual power of numbers, and they spend large amounts of money to buy the "better" license plate or a house with the better address. Others believe that by placing furniture in the proper arrangement, it will give them exceptional qualities. The belief systems of humans are immensely complicated and amazingly broad in scope, from superstitions, to cults to full blown religions; they are all based on a belief in the supernatural that is beyond the laws of natural physics as we know it

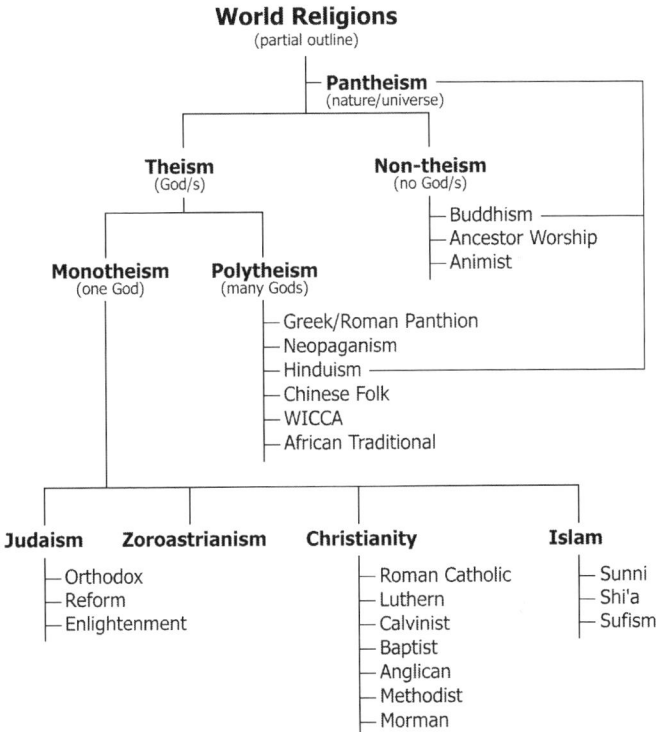

World Religions
(partial outline)

Pantheism
(nature/universe)

Theism
(God/s)

Non-theism
(no God/s)
— Buddhism
— Ancestor Worship
— Animist

Monotheism
(one God)

Polytheism
(many Gods)
— Greek/Roman Panthion
— Neopaganism
— Hinduism
— Chinese Folk
— WICCA
— African Traditional

Judaism   **Zoroastrianism**   **Christianity**   **Islam**
— Orthodox   — Roman Catholic   — Sunni
— Reform   — Luthern   — Shi'a
— Enlightenment   — Calvinist   — Sufism
                                   — Baptist
                                   — Anglican
                                   — Methodist
                                   — Morman

In America, we have come to think of religion as primarily synonymous with Christianity. We connect the idea of religion with a personal, living god; but, there are millions of people in the world who are religious, yet their religion does not involve gods.

There are two major divisions of religious systems, the theist and the non-theist religions. That is, those religions that have a god or gods are the theist faiths (Hindu, Islam, Christianity, etc.) The non-theist faiths include hundreds, perhaps thousands, of religions, and they include millions, if not billions, of believers with no specific gods.

The largest well known faith without a specific god is Buddhism. Buddhists focus on achieving "enlightenment" as a supernatural state, when the soul or life force no longer reincarnates. Gods are not necessary in this achievement. Believers must do the work themselves; they cannot be "saved" through belief in any god but only through actions considered "correct," and by believing in specific supernatural principles they can achieve the ultimate reward.

In addition to faiths such as Buddhism, there are literally thousands of animistic faiths. These are the ones based on belief in spiritual forces that interact with humans in some way. Some spirits are local and are only for the people of a particular area, city, island, or mountain range. Many of the Polynesian and other island peoples have faiths with spirits attributed to animals or volcanoes. Another type of non-theist religion is ancestor worship, where some quality of the person (soul) survives death and can then interact with the living. Ancestor worship often combines with animistic concepts and makes for a combined faith; in reality, the combination faith is the most common non-theist religious type.

Theism is where a supernatural god (or gods) controls, or at least could choose to have some control, over the life of a believer. Therefore, to be a theistic religion, followers have to believe that the agent to whom they pray is personally involved, or at least could affect their lives personally. Most theistic religions also include all the rules, structures and official documents that go with the religion, as administered under the authority of the designated holy men. (Unfortunately, I found remarkably few holy women.) Under this definition, I am not considering Deists to be members of a theistic religion. A Deist believes that there likely was a god that started everything (life, universe, etc.) but, like a clock maker, merely created it and is no longer involved in its operation. Most of America's founding fathers were Deists, as that was the time when little was known about natural science, and it was common to believe that something supernatural was necessary to create everything.

I think we can all benefit substantially from learning about the non-theist faiths, especially Buddhism, where living a high quality of social life is fundamental to achieving their version of salvation or enlightenment. Unlike the theists, for the most part, the non-theist religions are reasonably tolerant of other faiths. For example, the ancestor worshipers of Australia have no interest in condemning other believers or spreading their faith to other areas; it would make no sense, as their ancestors would have no knowledge about people from another area. But because this book is about the major problems with today's religions, I will be focusing on the theist religions. I have only included discussions of the non-theist religions when I think they shed valuable contrast or practical examples, compared to the religions with a god or gods.

The theist faiths are further divided into polytheism and monotheism. A prominent example of polytheism is the Hindu faith with many gods. Today various forms of polytheism have approximately one billion followers. In the west, we are most familiar with the older Greek and Roman gods where Zeus, Poseidon (my personal favorite,) and even the rulers of ancient Rome were worshipped as gods. Usually, where polytheism is practiced today one will find greater tolerance for other faiths and even a common merging of faiths into further combination faiths. Monotheism, which stands for one and only one god, is, on the other hand, far less tolerant, as discussed below.

Several large, contemporary religions claim to be monotheistic (have only one god), but it could be said that none of them actually has just one supernatural deity. If you ask an Islamic believer about Christianity, he is likely to say that the Christians believe in three gods -- God, Jesus and the Holy Ghost. Muslims seem to have one extremely powerful supernatural god called Allah; yet, they also have a supernatural, devil-like god, which they share with the Jews and, for that matter, with the Christians. Overall, it is complicated. But the Christians, the Muslims, and the Jews all call themselves "true" monotheistic religions, so I will take their word for it. It is these three major monotheistic religions of Christianity, Judaism, and Islam with which I am the most concerned.

As people have traveled and come in contact with other cultures, religions have merged; they have also evolved and become surprisingly complicated. So today, most religions have components of theism as well as non-theistic spirits, demons, and all kinds of combinations. You probably know someone that believes in ancestor worship as well as in a god. If contemporary television is any indicator, with all the programs looking for ghosts or seeing the dead, then spirits must be very popular.

Humans are astounding in their ability to form complex supernatural faiths. If you can think of something supernatural, there is probably a religion that incorporates that idea into its belief system. From talking snakes, flying horses, and sacred cows, to space visitors and crying statues, they are all popular components of many religions.

How Many Believe What?

I was surprised to discover just how prevalent religion is. The vast majority of all people in all cultures identify themselves as believing in some supernatural faith, god, or gods, all having to do with an after-life or reincarnation. Large Asian countries like China are officially nonreligious, but in reality Daoism, Confucianism and Buddhism are practiced widely. Of the nearly seven billion people on this planet almost 80 percent are identified with some religion. Half of them are now calling themselves monotheistic believers.

The two major monotheistic faiths are Christianity, with over two billion followers, and Islam, with well over a billion followers. Judaism has only 14 million believers, is the oldest of the surviving "desert" religions, and, because of its active political as well as strategic role in world wide issues, is very important. Milton states that there are over 1,500 separate "denominations" of religions. David Gibbons identifies 28 major, and what he calls alternative, religions, which have nearly a million followers each. Even the Church of Satan and WICCA each claim 20 to 800 thousand current members. There are thousands of current religions and nearly that many different gods. The top 15 religions and nonreligious groups including the number of adherents are:

1. Christianity: 2.1 billion
2. Islam: 1.5 billion

3.	Secular/Nonreligious/Atheist:	1.1 billion
4.	Hinduism:	900 million
5.	Chinese traditional religion:	394 million
6.	Buddhism:	376 million
7.	Primal-indigenous:	300 million
8.	African Traditional & Diasporic:	100 million
9.	Sikhism:	23 million
10.	Juche:	19 million
11.	Spiritism:	15 million
12.	Judaism:	14 million
13.	Baha'i:	7 million
14.	Jainism:	4.2 million
15.	Shinto:	4 million

Note that the third largest identifiable group in this list are those who call themselves nonreligious.

The timeline that I have studied goes back further than what most people think of as the age of religion (4,000 to 6,000 years). I am interested in what social anthropologists think about early humans, and about how their myths, tribal superstitions, and legends probably evolved into the major religions of today. It seems that some type of faith system has been documented all the way back to the Cro-Magnon burial sites in the Czech Republic some 25,000 years ago. Most anthropologists believe that faith and language both came along at about the same time, so the advent of religion likely goes back much further, possibly 80,000 years. Therefore, we have a long history of belief in spirits, demons, gods and the supernatural. There's no doubt that, over the vast history of human existence, nearly all humans have believed in the supernatural world, and these beliefs have been a significant part of human evolution.

It is common in American English to capitalize the word God, but, because there are so many gods, I have chosen not to capitalize the word unless it is in reference to a named god. For the most part, the word god means a supernatural deity of some religion. That does not warrant capitalization any more than the words spirit, ghost or demon. When I refer to Christianity's God I will capitalize it. When I use the term supernatural, it is not meant to be derogatory. It is in an effort to be clear that those who are followers of a religion have a belief either in a deity that has powers beyond those of our natural world as we now understand it, or they have a belief in spirits or in a supernatural quality that is achieved by specific rituals or acts. In short, the theists believe that a deity can suspend the natural laws of the universe, which is what I mean by supernatural. The non-theists believe that particular superhuman things exist, such as ghosts and spirits, and that those agents interact with humans in supernatural ways.

What is surprising to me is that the vast majority of people believe in powers that are outside of natural physics. They really do believe that there are supernatural powers. I realize that I should have known this all along; somehow I thought that it was just something from the past and I would find the majority of modern people all over the world are mostly practical, would agree with the scientific approach to the unknown, and that horror and science fiction was just that -- fiction. What I have found is that the majority of people in the world believe in spirits, demons, ghosts and gods of one kind or another.

Most of the theistic religions have gods that are believed to have the ability to know everything about everyone (omniscient) all at the same time; they are all powerful (omnipotent); they are everywhere at once (omnipresent); and they have created everything except themselves. In addition, there are thousands of these gods, some with thousands, millions, or even billions of believers. To say that god is just another name for nature, and that the universe is my church, is not the kind of religion I'm talking about. From here on, I'm talking about religions based upon supernatural gods that, according to their believers, can hear their prayers, suspend the laws of physics, regularly interact with humans, and perform miracles.

The next section, Questions about Religion, discusses many of the common questions people ask about religion. I have tried to provide answers to each question, but when it comes to religion and beliefs, many things cannot be factually answered, as there is no way of knowing what the truth is. I make no claim to know any "truths." In fact, I'm quite sure I don't know any.

The third section describes what I regard as the Big Problem with religion. The major monotheistic religions seem to be stuck in the past with a set of documents that cause constant limitations on these faiths' getting along, on solving pressing world problems, and even constraining their members from being "culturally moral people."

In the fourth section, I propose solutions that we can all implement to respond to these big problems. Solutions to large, enduring problems are difficult to implement; yet there are essential starting points we can all take on a personal and daily basis that will help move us in a positive direction and, who knows? They might just save all of humanity!

Part Two - - Questions About Religion

Why do most people believe in a religion?

The first and simplest answer to the question, "Why do people believe in a religion?" is that, as children, they were taught religious beliefs by their parents or some other significant adult. Children's brains are open to fantasies and magic. They believe what they are told, so superstitions, Santa Clause, invisible friends, and a baby god born of a virgin, are just a natural part of their childhood. Being taught what to believe as children clearly explains why children believe the same as their parents, and why in each country or region of the world, for the most part, all the people believe the same religion. It is also interesting to learn that most religions are taught to children in schools and in community forums; everyone gets the same message and ends up believing in the same religion. What religion you identify with depends on where you were born and how religious your parents or schools were. Gods do not choose their followers; people usually do not choose their religion; parents are responsible for it all.

Many, if not most, countries have an official religion taught and practiced throughout the country. In many countries, the schools, adding to parental influence as they take on the role of education for the community, are primarily religious training institutions and secondarily, if at all, educational institutions. That is, true education -- learning to question all things, to analyze, to do research, and to reflect objectively about things -- is often not taught if it collides with religious faith. Religion, on the other hand, is usually not taught as an intellectual topic that would introduce children to many religions and provide the opportunity to learn about their similarities and differences. Doing so would allow them to make a decision about which, if any, is right for them.

All religions that wish to maintain or expand their numbers are committed to indoctrinating their children into their faith. Babies are not born with a faith; they are taught what to believe just like they are taught a language. There is no such thing as a Jewish child or a Christian child; they are only children of Jewish or Christian parents. Children are unable to obtain a religion until their brains have developed to a point where they can understand the complex concepts of mortality, reincarnation, and salvation. Many researchers believe that, as a child matures, his or her brain becomes especially adapted to accept supernatural ideas, including religion.

In addition to this first and simplest answer, there is a lot of research reporting on how the human brain has developed over the past 500,000 years and how primitive tribes used superstitions and, later, more formal religions, to help them stay alive. Many researchers believe religion has helped primitive communities remain strong as a group, and "cultural evolution" has resulted in modern human societies with a natural tendency to believe in supernatural agents. I will spend more time on this later but, for now, the main point is that most children are taught to believe in an invisible god along with many amazing stories about supernatural events and about what happens after death.

It is intriguing to see how religions have spread and why people now have a religion that is different from their ancestors. David Gibbons' book, Faiths and Religions of the World, has a four page fold-out showing how the present world religions have spread around the globe. The Spanish conquests of much of South America, followed by the Portuguese and the British incursions into Australia and the South Pacific, are notable examples of where people got their current religion. In almost all cases, religions were spread by the sword in search of gold, spices, and power. The monotheistic religions of Christianity and Islam have a particularly strong tradition of making sure that those under their political power adopt their religion. These conquered people had some form of their own religion, but now most of them have adopted the religion of the conquering country. In the past, and to a lesser extent now, this is how religion has spread and changed in most areas.

We still see new religions developing, but the current trend is more toward the polarization of two or three major world-wide religions. At present, the Islamic faith is the fastest growing religion in the world. The conflict of these "mega" religions is one of the major problems of the world today and will be discussed in the third section.

Why don't most people get over their supernatural beliefs when they become adults?

Some people do outgrow their supernatural beliefs, but most people compartmentalize their religious beliefs and their rational thoughts into separate conceptual structures. Unlike Santa Claus and invisible friends, where our adult society encourages those beliefs to fade out as the child matures, religion is supported as an acceptable adult belief system. That is, religious beliefs are considered different from childhood fantasies that we outgrow and from thoughts about everyday practical problems requiring logic and thought. It is as though religion is fixed in rigid form and that it continues to exist in a part of the brain that does not question or think about the logic of the beliefs. There seems to be a particularly special place in the brain where religious beliefs just seem to fit. Religious thoughts in this particular place are not questioned. Religious thoughts often make people feel good or at least secure in their understanding of their experiences; believers reward themselves for having such thoughts and for the comfortable way they make them feel.

I was asked the other day if I was "raised Catholic." What the person was actually asking was if I had a set of childhood experiences that would have provided me a specific set of rituals and beliefs that are unique to the Catholic religion. It is as if, once exposed to these religious experiences, I would be permanently attached to that religion, and those beliefs would still be available for activation. To some extent, children are imprinted with the faith that they are taught, and it automatically goes into that brain area reserved for religious beliefs; it is not usually questioned or further evaluated as they become adults.

You may have heard the statement, "Once a Catholic, always a Catholic." Religion often becomes a cultural force as well as a faith. Judaism is a good example; many of the religion-based customs and activities of those believing as a Jew are woven into their total daily life, with food constraints, clothing requirements, and various other everyday practices, which seem more cultural than religious.

In a society like ours in America, it is customary to protect religious beliefs from any open discussion or questioning; they are not to be disturbed in that special place in the brain. In this country, it is just "wrong" to discuss critically or analytically one's own or another's religion or to say anything negative about any system of faith. In many other societies, it is more than just wrong to say anything negative or challenge the official religion. In fact, blasphemy is still punishable by death in many places. To even suggest that a person does not totally agree with the official faith can result in loss of employment and social isolation or worse. To a lesser degree, for people to be anything but religious (Christian) in America often makes them subject to persecution and social rejection, and they are often made uncomfortable when participating in routine community life. For many of us who are concerned about the freedom of our country, the taboo on intellectually-based critique of religion is one of the biggest problems facing our country and one that needs to change.

If you ask a lot of people, as I have, why they think people believe in a religion, you get answers such as, "Religion comforts people in their suffering and fear of death," or "Religion explains things we cannot otherwise explain." These seem "logical," but when you look carefully into them, you still end up questioning why one should believe in an invisible god when there is no evidence that it exists, or asking why believing the stories about supernatural explanations for natural phenomenon is actually all that comforting to modern, intelligent people. Yet, it is clear that the faithful get a lot of comfort from their faith, that their religion is very important to them, and that they do not want to question it or think rationally about it.

The reasons people have a religious belief system are numerous. Guy Harrison describes 50 of them and says repeatedly that believers are not interested in debating the logic of their reasons for believing. Personally, I think believing in a supernatural god and participating in the religious community just makes them happy, and, to a certain extent, that is a perfectly legitimate reason to believe.

People attribute positive things that happen in their lives to supernatural gods after praying for a good outcome. When good things happen, it reinforces their conviction that something, or someone, is looking out for them. This "random motivator" is a very strong reason to keep believing, because it seems to work part of the time. As any behavioral psychologist knows, an occasional random motivator is the strongest means to keep a subject conditioned to a particular behavior. On the other hand, when bad things happen to believers, they blame it on the government, other humans, or on themselves, but seldom on their god. Here, I understand the word praying to mean a direct, personal communication with a god. Prayer is also often thought to be a summons to get the attention of a god or a spirit, although most religions believe that their god knows everything and hears everything said by everyone; prayer is a special communication initiated by the human.

Another factor that keeps adults believing is what I call the "spirituality awe factor." Without necessarily thinking terribly deeply about the scientific reasons why some things are so fantastic, beautiful and complicated, we are emotionally moved by them. A beautiful sunset, a clear star-filled night, and the complexity of life itself are all awe-inspiring. These things are truly breathtaking, and it is easy to say, "I see god in all of them." They were created for me by my god. A more reasonable and accurate explanation, but requiring a lot more effort to understand, is also available. Pollution and water vapor cause our beautiful sunsets, and our little galaxy is filled with burning balls of nuclear fusion giving off light that takes thousands of years to get to us. Yes, life is immensely complicated, but it got that way based upon a system of random accidents that all operate on the natural selection principle that was clearly stated by Darwin and is now accepted by most thoughtful people. So, if accurate and logical reasons for the inspiring things around us exist, why aren't these answers good enough? Is there some basic need for a creator god to be involved?

Let us step back in time and consider how we got to this point, where belief is so common and seems to feel natural. Boyer and Atran have written extensively on how social evolution has conditioned humans to accept religion as a useful "group selection" tool. They conclude that this conditioning has made those groups accepting superstition and tribal religion more successful in staying alive than those who do not. Those who don't accept tribal superstitions become less successful and eventually die off. This social development is similar to biological natural selection, but it operates on a faster scale. The brain learns over thousands of generations that believing in one or more supernatural agents is the normal or natural thing to do, and it does not need to be logical. The supernatural belief provides comfort, reduces fear of death, and explains the unexplainable to people without ever really being questioned; modern scientific knowledge was not available until very recently, so those beliefs were, in their own way, quite "logical" for the time.

It seems that the modern human brain has been conditioned over thousands or maybe even millions of years of evolution to accept some ideas or customs without critical thought. These ideas have been called memes, and they are seen as easy to accept without question. It is as if the idea, or the superstition in this case, has a life of its own. If the meme benefits the individual then it is carried on to the next generation and is reproduced, similar to how a gene in the body is sometimes slightly changed as it is replicated. The new version is even more successful for the new generation, and that modification is then passed on.

The fundamental ideas of most religions fall into such meme categories. These are systems of shared beliefs and ideas that exist in every culture. The evolution of these universal ideas is why it is so easy to believe, for example, that aliens from other planets are here, ghosts are real, spirits and angels exist, and that a supernatural invisible god is looking out for us. In short, these ideas have been evolving as long as there has been language. Our modern brains now accept these memes, and they get put away in their specific places; thus we find ourselves watching TV programs about ghosts, spirits, aliens, and mind readers, and it all can easily seem perfectly normal and even plausible.

Many anthropologists and biologists believe that these long standing superstitions have been prominent in protecting humans from natural enemies, including other humans. Therefore, a psychological evolution of ideas, or memes, has occurred in our brains making many ideas, including the acceptance of a god or religion, perfectly natural. Customary superstitious behaviors, such as listening to the spirits in the wind or watching out for a demon in the forest, make believers more careful. Thus, they are more likely to survive, they tell their "close call" stories to others, and their children believe these stories and are also subsequently more careful. While these memes are not really similar to genes, where biological evolution has shaped them by natural selection, the analogy is useful to explain why we are so drawn to fantasies about ghosts, demons, witches, and supernatural god(s). In short, to believe in the supernatural is normal because our brains are conditioned to believe. Those of us who do not believe in such things are the "psychological mutations."

Modern humans can simultaneously function in both the rational world of logic and in the comforting, non-rational world of supernatural beliefs, all of which fit easily into their historically adapted minds. It is this evolution of our brains that makes it easy for us to compartmentalize the "believable" childhood stories of a religion separate from our reasoning and logical processing of our direct experience of the real world. It is thus "natural" to believe in gods, spirits, and demons; this comes easily and feels right for most people, even though they are also able to think rationally about other subjects. This is how many scientists who use rational logic in their professions can separate their faith from their work. Though rigorously demanding of evidence in their work, they don't attempt to rigorously justify their faith; they just accept it and believe it.

I'm not suggesting that there is any inherent problem with believing in the supernatural and, as far as I know, some or even all such things might be real. Most of the world does believe in some religious structure. Many religions provide a framework for how to live a successful life. Most religions have doctrines for answering questions about creation, about where the universe came from. As long as these beliefs do not impede intellectual growth and investigative science from producing useful improvements in both knowledge and quality of human life, they may cause no problems.

Most religions also have common references as to how we should treat each other. Again, most of these are positive, and they merely reinforce common-sense social norms, again causing no harm and often bringing on a lot of good. In addition, there is evidence that prayer, "speaking directly to god," is good for a person. Dr. Robert Buckman says, "In psychiatric terminology, the act of thinking about a problem in a beneficial way that reduces the traumatic effect of the problem is called a coping strategy." It is this coping strategy that many people use to handle the stress of everyday life or traumatic events. Today, as I was writing this, we had a terrible shooting of four police officers at a coffee shop in a rural town just east of Tacoma, Washington. Within hours of the event a "prayer vigil" was set up, and hundreds of people attended. They were there to cope with this terrible event in their normally tranquil town; they found comfort in payer and in the presence of similar like-minded people, all trying to make some sense of such a violent act which left nine children and four spouses without a parent or partner. Many will find comfort in thinking that this senseless execution was part of some greater plan they can not understand; others will find comfort in just talking about it with their god. Overall, they are coping with a tragedy in a natural way that feels right, and, for them, prayer works.

Why isn't everybody religious?

Why do some people -- about 15 percent in the US and nearly 50 percent in Europe -- not belong to any religion and say they are not religious?

First, let me describe what I mean by "nonreligious." When you ask people if they are religious, some will respond with something like, "I was raised a Lutheran but I'm not religious any more," or they may say something like, "I don't attend any church." When pressed further about their beliefs, some say, "Well I'm an agnostic but not really religious." Like many of these people, I used to say I was an agnostic. It seemed like a good way to avoid making a decision as to whether I did or did not believe in a god. The term agnostic was created by Thomas Huxley in 1869 to describe something that was, in his opinion, "unknowable" and therefore could not be described or known to exist. Dan Barker the Co-President of the Freedom from Religion Foundation (FFRF) defines this term as someone who refuses to accept as a fact any account for which there is insufficient evidence. This does not apply just to religion or belief in a god(s). It seems that, in the United States over the years, this term has come to mean one who is not committed to believing or disbelieving in a supernatural god. In essence, this is "fence-sitting," which frees one from having to answer the question, "Do you believe in a god?"

Austin Cline defines the term agnostic in a typically dualistic manner: *"Obviously, if theism is a belief in a God and atheism is a lack of a belief in a God, no third position or middle ground is possible. A person can either believe or not believe in a God. Therefore, our previous definition of atheism has made an impossibility out of the common usage of agnosticism to mean "neither affirming nor denying a belief in God."* These days, in reporting formal research on this issue, agnostics will usually be included in the same grouping as atheists and/or nonreligious people. Now, I realize that saying I am agnostic was a little like the soon-to-be mother saying she does not know if she is pregnant or not. It only takes time, or a small test, to find out or, in my case, just thinking about it more seriously. After a little thought, it was obvious that I did not believe in a god. You can continue to sit on the fence only if you don't think about the question. Do you believe in a god? If the answer is yes, then you are a theist; if the answer is no then you are an atheist.

Another reason I think people have for identifying as agnostic is that they don't want to be labeled an atheist. Being an atheist is just "bad." I'm not sure why, but I get the impression from my society and culture that it is just a bad thing to say.

At this point, the word atheist needs to be clarified. An atheist is one who does not believe in the existence of a supernatural god. Everyone is born an atheist; we learn our religions just like our language. Some children are taught a second language and some are taught a religion. If a person does not believe there is a god, it does not mean that the person "believes" that there is no god. Let me say this again because it is so easy to be misunderstood; "not believing" does not mean that a person believes there is no god. Here, believing is the key word. Atheism is not a religion or any other kind of belief structure; it simply means that a person does not believe in a god. A lack of belief is not a belief.

Carl Sagan talked a lot about wanting there to be aliens in outer space, but the bottom line was that there is no evidence they existed; therefore, he had to say that, at this point, there is no reason for believing that they exist. The same is true for many who call themselves atheists, including myself. As soon as there is some reason or evidence to believe in a supernatural god, we may change our minds, but until then, we do not have any reason to say that gods exist. I hope this is clear, that an atheist is what people are called who don't believe in a supernatural god.

Now, some people say they "know" or believe that there is no such thing as a god. They believe that there are no gods; they have faith that there are no gods. Boy, that sounds almost like those who believe that there IS a god because they are religious and have faith. Those who simply don't believe in a god are sometimes called "soft, negative, or lower case atheists." Those who believe that there is no god are then called, hard, positive or upper case, Atheists. One author calls them "anti-theists." I call these people the angry atheists, and they should not be confused with merely being an atheist. In my experience, those that have a firm "belief" that there is no god(s) are often adamant that others adopt their belief, much the same as those who believe in a particular religion want to proselytize their belief. Personally, I don't know of any good reason to believe there is a god, and therefore I do not think there is a god. But I learn new things all the time; give me some rational evidence that there is a god and I'll change my mind. Now that does not mean I'm undecided, because until I have documented, repeatable evidence that a god exists, I don't think one does. This makes me a "soft, or lower case atheist."

Now it is also true in the strictest sense that millions of religious people are atheists, such as all the Buddhists, the animistic followers, and all the ancestor worshipers who do not believe in any gods. In reality, gods, and especially the monotheistic gods, are a relatively new invention. Religions existed for thousands of years before belief in gods evolved. They were based on supernatural agents called daemons, spirits, and dead relatives, all having supernatural powers over humans. In ancient Greek mythology, daemons were quite varied in their roles, with both negative and positive qualities. The word, daemon, and its religious concept, morphed into the more negative, malignant notion of "demons" as evil spirits in early Christianity. Again, what most Americans mean when they say they are an atheist is that they reject any supernatural faith and base their life on demonstrated reality.

In an attempt to find a new label for people who do not have fixed beliefs in any religious concept, David Eller uses the term discredism. Discredism is based upon the Latin prefix dis or 'apart,' and the Latin credere for 'to believe.' Therefore, it means, simply, no belief or without belief. I think this might be a good way to describe someone who does not have religious beliefs; inventing a new term might get away from all the negative baggage that goes with the term atheist. I think I can live with calling myself a discredist, but I find it simpler just to say I'm a nonbeliever; it gives me a chance to explain.

The word belief, like religion, is hard to explain, but fundamentally it is the psychological state of holding a thesis or a premise to be true. In practice, a belief is what we "know" to be true without any evidence, or as is often stated, a belief is something we want to be true. Or as the Bible says, *"Faith is the substance of things hoped for, the evidence of things not seen."* (Hebrews 11:1)

Now, in an effort to explain why some people clearly say they are nonreligious, let's look at some sub groups. It seems that there are three distinct groups of people who describe themselves as not religious. The first group, including myself, is of those who were not taught as children to believe in any supernatural gods. David Eller calls us in his first book "natural atheists" because we were never indoctrinated into a belief system and were free to think about it rationally. As more and more young adults raise their children in a rational world without teaching faith, we will see this group grow, faster, for now, in Europe than in the United States. Overall, though, I suspect we are still a small minority.

The important point about members of this group is that they are usually open to the possibility of supernatural gods. In my case, I would love to meet a god, or even to learn that there is documented evidence that one exists. Just imagine the headlines and TV coverage it would create and what we could learn from a god. Who knows what will be discovered in the future. To a human living 10,000 years ago, any one of us with a cell phone would be a god with magical powers. While I'm now comfortable with the label nonbeliever or discredist, it just means I do not currently believe in a supernatural god or any other supernatural agents.

Being a child with parents who did not teach religion gives that child a unique perspective. Maybe our special brain spot never gets developed, or it is still sitting empty, waiting for something to be put into the space. I had the unusual opportunity to be taught to argue about everything, not from a point of view of knowing in the "religious" sense of knowing, but in just thinking about things and trying to get across why I think the way I do. My wife says that I used to love to argue so much that sometimes I would switch sides and take a more extreme point of view. I don't know if I ever did that, but the idea sounds like fun. I no longer argue very much about things, but

I still think about them, and I try to find answers to questions that interest me.

The point of view that you really don't know anything for sure, yet you are free to think about everything as rationally as you can, is quite different from that of my religious friends who tell me that they know something because they have a belief or faith, a "truth" on which to base things. Sometimes I'm a little jealous, as it would be gratifying to actually know something for sure. But then I think about all the fun I have questioning everything and learning new things all the time. I'm very happy being a nonbeliever who does not know anything for sure.

A second group of people who are not religious is composed of those who have become uncomfortable with their faith and now reject what they were taught. This seems to be a large group who identify themselves as currently not belonging to a religion. Some have left their faith because of disenchantment with it. Perhaps they were abused by their priest, or were made to feel different from their peers by their parents, or maybe they just got tired of all the rituals in their particular version of religion. Many are quiet about leaving their faith, but, when pressed, make it clear that they want no part of organized religion again. Yet, they also do not want to make a scene or take the chance of being labeled an atheist. Others include those who seem to go in and out of religions as though they were changing jobs. They seem to easily join another religion if something attracts them into it, as long as the new religion is different from whatever made them uncomfortable with the old one. These people were merely unhappy with some particular aspect of their faith, and they drifted away. If a compelling reason comes along for them to participate again, they are likely to move into another group of believers.

Another portion of this group is the "angry atheists." They are out to get even for all the pain and suffering they went through before leaving their faith. This is where a lot of the negative talk about religion by nonbelievers comes from. These atheists often act just like the faithful, committed to pushing what they now believe about non-belief onto everyone else. While it is easy to find a lot of reasons to be angry at most large organized religions, bashing and making fun of believers while stating an equally strong unfounded disbelief in a god is of little value in changing the believer's mind, and it demonstrates the same behavior that is being criticized. Here I'm only talking about bashing someone for their belief in a supreme being. I think there are many legitimate reasons for being angry about religious behavior which leads to abuse, hatred, violence and ignorance, about which I have much more to say later. There is a vast difference between just believing in a god, and living out a hate filled religious life that is based upon abusing other people.

The third, and likely the largest, group of those who call themselves nonreligious are those who try to understand the logic of their childhood faith but ultimately cannot fit it into the reality of a reasonable universe. They think about the illogic of believing in an invisible god, or how impossible reincarnation would be, or how silly the stories of their religion truly are, and they conclude that they don't need it in their life to be a happy, successful person. This is where modern science, Darwin's brilliant discovery, and "common sense" finally brakes into that compartment of the brain where childhood religion is stored, and just cleans house.

I suspect this is a much larger group of people than we realize, but they just ignore the whole issue because it is so socially unacceptable in most societies to talk about it or to admit publicly that they have no religious belief. They are often more like Deists, where they believe that there might have been a god that started all of this, but that god doesn't involve itself with humans, and people don't get into a "personal relationship" with such a god. Similarly, these people do not follow any scriptures or join any organized church. Because this is, for the most part, an invisible group, I have no solid documentation about how large this group might be; but several authors who have done independent surveys suggest this to be a much larger portion of our society than our current national surveys would indicate.

It is understandable that people in America would be reluctant to admit that they are not religious. As a minority group, atheists are commonly thought of as the least desirable and most persecuted of all groups. Even immediately after 9/11 the rejection of atheists was still higher than for Muslims. A 2006 study by the University of Minnesota found that 47.6 percent of the respondents said that an atheist is the last person on earth they want to see their child marry. This is considerably higher than for any other minority group. This prejudice and open discrimination can even be seen in social service organizations, for example, the Philanthropic Educational Organization (P.E.O.) is a sisterhood, with a mission of promoting educational opportunities for women and has chapters all across the United States. This is not a church-based organization, but there is only one minority of women they do not want in their sisterhood; the atheist is not welcome to join and help other women. We are not talking about identified sex-offenders, rapist or murderers. We are talking about good, caring, moral people who just do not believe in a supernatural god. Our prisons are not full of atheists; in fact, quite the opposite is true. There is no rational reason to believe atheists are any less trustworthy or dangerous than anyone else. It is no wonder that people keep their unbelief a secret; they don't want to endure the rejection and discrimination that could affect their employment status or even lead to violence against them.

Why are there so many religious people in the United States?

Why is there such a large percentage of religious people in the United States, and why are the more extreme fundamentalist or evangelical protestant groups of the Christian faith growing the fastest?

These are two of the most difficult questions to answer because it is clear that, in the United States, there is a large group of literate, knowledgeable people who have access to modern information and who are generally reasonable about most things in their lives. Yet, when it comes to religion, they are passionate and religious; Evangelical Christianity is especially popular. Some researchers believe it is because the United States has made religion an open option, a foundational matter of free choice. Therefore, competition among religions has flourished. By comparison, it is certainly true that, while England has an official state church which can seem rather boring to the people of England, the US has a wide variety of churches, literally, on every corner. Perhaps the competition along with the freedom to choose has increased membership.

Another answer is that social pressure to remain identified as a religious person, and especially as a Christian person, is strong in this country. Among the faithful, the term Christian has become synonymous with trustworthy and just being a good person. For the most part, this is true; there are a lot of good, thoughtful, and caring people in

America who consider themselves Christians. These "moderate" Christians often do not belong to a church, they do not follow their holy scriptures literally, and they have never read much, if any, of their holy book. They call themselves Christian because that is what they were raised to say when asked about religion, and overall they live what they consider a "Christian" life. Being religious is not the same as participating in a religious organization. A 2003 Harris poll found that only a minority of the public (36%) attends a religious service once a month or more often, with only about a quarter (26%) attending every week.

Overall, it is just easier to believe and to keep religion in that safe brain compartment than to analyze the logic of the faith. Therefore, most Americans just continue to go along. They get a lot of comfort from belonging, it feels right to them (our memes are working), and it would be very unpopular to question what we are not supposed to talk about. I'm sure it is a lot more complicated than this, but in my simple way of looking at things, this makes reasonable sense. It is just easier to be like our neighbors than it is to question and think about what we are doing and saying.

The vast majority of Christian churches do a lot of good things, but most prominent in answering this question is that they offer a lot of pleasure to their members. The organized churches of America provide a valuable social structure to our society. Belonging is important in our United States culture. Finding a safe place to socialize, to find friends, and to just enjoy being with others of a similar mind set is very important. Much of this social pleasure is provided by our organized religious groups. Traveling through many areas of rural America, one will often notice that a church or two are the only buildings in a community that provide the venue for social gatherings.

A 1990 survey showed evangelical or "born–again" membership to be growing at 42 percent, the highest rate of growth of all identifiable religious groups. In my research, I only found two authors who have dealt with the second part of this question as to why Christian Evangelical religious groups are growing so fast.

Stark and Finke explain it in terms of supply and demand theory. In America, which is generally affluent by world standards, we can usually afford to get what we want. Not only can we get what we want, but we tend to believe that we get what we pay for. In other words, if we pay more for something, we get more, and we get a better product. They describe the growth of the Evangelical religious groups in the same way. In essence, the product that is being purchased is a belief in a positive position in an afterlife. By belonging to a more expensive church, not only in money, but in time, extreme actions, and costly involvement, the member is more likely to achieve salvation or even a better salvation. In this way, the churches that seem to be extreme or "expensive" to belong to and participate in are becoming more popular because they are more likely to provide the bigger and better pay-off. I have no way of knowing if this is really a factor in the growth of these churches, but it sounds like an engaging answer, and it is the only one I have found. I suspect a careful look at other sociological factors in the communities where growth is happening might shed a less market-oriented, "fun" reason, but I like this one.

Another trend in American religion is that of the "megachurch," those institutions with well over 2000 weekly attendees. The major megachurches are combination protestant denominations including Assembly of God, Lutherans, Presbyterians, Baptists and Methodists. They are developed around charismatic leaders like Joel Osteen in Houston, with over 30,000 members; Rick Warren at Saddleback Church in California, with 22,000 members; and Bill Hybels of Willow Creek Church in Chicago, with 19,000 members. They are far less interested in the doctrinal differences between protestant denominations than they are in promoting the common fundamentalism of Christianity. The old differences between denominations have melted away here; many members do not identify themselves as members of a denomination, but rather as a member of a particular megachurch.

These institutions appeal to the upwardly mobile middle class with popular music and entertainment as big draw features. While not traditional in their identification as a protestant denomination, they are very fundamentally evangelical in their messages. The Bible is the focus, and a lot of literal interpretation is the message. Every major urban community now has, or is growing, an evangelical megachurch. Americans seem to like the modern spacious facilities, the big congregations, the big media productions, the excitement of belonging to something big, all of which are significant factors in American middle class life.

More recently, in May of 2009, Insight Express conducted a national survey of 1,051 adults for Parade Magazine. When asked if they consider themselves religious, 45 percent said yes. When asked if they were spiritual rather than religious, 24 percent said yes, and only 14 percent said they were neither religious nor spiritual. Forty percent of them said that religion is the source of truth, and 69 percent stated they believe in God. Seventy-five percent thought it was important to raise children with a religious upbringing.

It is clear that we are still a very religious country. What seems to be happening is that traditional dogma and ritual associated with Catholics, protestant denominations, and even Jewish followers, are being adapted into what is now being called "spirituality." While it is true that the latest national surveys of religion in America has shown an increase in the nonreligious category, especially along the east and west coasts, overall, religion seems to continue as a strong pattern of American life.

Why is it important to keep "Church" and "State" totally separate?

We are very fortunate to live in a country where our founding fathers had the foresight to separate religion from government. The "wall of separation," as Thomas Jefferson called it, where there shall be no interference by government in the affairs of religion and religion shall not interfere in the business of government, is one of the principles that make the United States a great country. In reality, this is a crucial protection for everyone. It is just as important for those who are religious as it is for those who do not have a belief in a supernatural agent. Thomas Jefferson, said, *"State churches that use government power to support themselves and force their views on persons of other faiths undermine all our civil rights . . . Erecting the 'wall of separation between church and state', is absolutely essential in a free society."*

The First Amendment to the US Constitution says, "Congress shall make no law respecting an establishment of religion, or prohibiting the free exercise thereof...." It is all about freedom -- in America, we are free to believe, and we are also free to not believe. Freedom to believe in different religions is not really freedom unless it also includes the freedom to not believe. Our laws and government are for everyone. It does not matter what a person's faith is or is not; our government gives everyone the right to believe and practice their beliefs any way they wish. No religion is advocated or established by the founding documents of this country. We are not a Christian-based or any other religion-based country; we are a secular country.

Even Jesus Christ seems to agree that church and state should be separate. He states, *"Render unto Caesar the things which are Caesar's and unto God the things that are God's."* (Matt. 22.17) Several historians, including Karen Armstrong, have explained that many of the interpretations modern Christians have taken so literally from scripture were from ideas intended merely as general advice, and that a clear separation between practical, or political, and religious concepts were the norm at the time. Things that dealt with practical matters were logically based, and things that dealt with spiritual matters were religion-based; the two did not need to be combined or be rationalized. Nevertheless, in many fundamental Christian communities in the U.S., it has become common to allow religious elements to infiltrate public schools, government meetings, and even legal proceedings. We all need to be diligent and vocal in keeping church and state separate; it is the law, and it is good for everyone.

While the inclusion of religion in social activities in our American society is not against the law per se, as it is when it is injected into government and public educational activity, it nevertheless does seem inappropriate. I'm often uncomfortable when an invocation (summoning divine intervention) or a prayer, which is usually of a Christian nature, is added to a totally secular event. It seems only polite to be respectful of all attendees at such events, of those of differing beliefs as well as of those who are nonbelievers, by not including such public prayer. This does not mean that people at such secular events cannot be "publicly grateful" or in remembrance of former deceased participants. But this can and should be done without involving religion.

In some faith systems, separation from government is a nonstarter. There is no doubt about keeping government and religion separated in the Islamic faith; it is not so. There is no separation; in fact, every political and legal system is required to be based upon the Qur'an or the Sunna (secondary document of rules of conduct), and politics, governments and laws within an Islamic country are all based first upon holy scripture as written over 1400 years ago. Ibn Warraq, writing on the nature of Islam says, "Right from the beginning, the Muslims formed a community that was at once political and religious, with the Prophet himself as head of state." As Americans, this Islamic belief that religion and political control go hand in hand should be particularly concerning, given that Islam is the fastest growing religion, including its surprising growth in this country. Conflicts are already common in Europe over Muslim inroads into policy and government activity. It is clear that if a majority of Muslims have their way, religion will become the foundation of governing policy. In France, where Islam is becoming a growing social force, there are already conflicts about allowing fully veiled women in public places, and some are trying to legislate against fundamentalists' religious attire.

While it seems silly for there to be an atheist organization, because it may seem to be about not believing or organizing about "nothing", there is an extraordinarily effective organization with the cause of "protecting the constitutional principle of the separation of state and church" called the **Freedom From Religion Foundation** (FFRF), www.//ffrf.org. They have successfully taken legal action to eliminate religious activity in public schools, government proceedings and where public money is involved. There is nothing trivial about protecting the right to be free to not believe, to be protected from religious abuses directed at those outside of a religious group, or of the constitutional validity of separating church from state.

Why "under god"?

After nearly 150 years of clear separation of church and state, why did we add a religious statement to our Pledge of Allegiance?

As best as I can tell, our country in the early 1950s was experiencing a lot of fear about Communism. Many were pushing for a clear statement that we were decidedly different from the "godless" political system of Communism that some were so afraid would infiltrate our country. Under President Eisenhower in 1954, with all the whipped up fear of Communism known as McCarthyism, Congress added the statement "under God" to our Pledge Allegiance at the urging of the Knights of Columbus and other religious organizations. In June of 2002, the "under God" wording was challenged in the Ninth Circuit Court of Appeals, where the ruling came down that "under God" is identical to saying a nation under Jesus, a nation under Vishnu, a nation under Zeus, or a nation under no god, so the Pledge stood as-is and was not appealed.

This seems silly to me, that saying "under god" is actually the same as saying under no god. Why say anything? But that is what the court decided, and it stands for now. Even though our Congress and courts made this decision about the Pledge of Allegiance, that does not make us a Christian country or any other kind of formally defined religious country. Our Constitution still clearly separates church and state, and we all, as free-thinking citizens, need to resist any movement by our legislators, our courts, or our public schools toward promoting any faith. As Thomas Jefferson said, "Question with Boldness."

Should religion be taught in our public schools?

The answer is unequivocally yes! What should not be taught is "faith," the indoctrination of students in any particular religion. When we fail to teach one of the major things that affect the daily operations of most of the world and that controls how most people on earth think and make decisions, we end up with an ignorant population. It is particularly valuable for any educated person to understand what religions teach and why followers of the major faiths make the decisions that they do.

Why do terrorists, as we call them, blow themselves up in an attempt to kill as many "infidels" as possible? Why are some governments, like Somalia, unable to maintain any degree of stability? Why do we in the United States make the decisions about foreign aid that we do? Why are some health procedures not allowed or some research not funded that could make a substantial improvement in the health of people all over the world?

Religion is always at the center of the answers to these questions. Every educated citizen needs to be well schooled in the social and political consequences of all major religions. We need to have our children grow up understanding the major religions of this world and knowing that it is okay to talk about them. It is also okay for each of them to believe or to not believe. One of the most powerful things we can do to make our world safe in the future is teach our youth about religion.

It is not my intention in saying all of this to somehow eliminate anyone's belief in a deity. Again, it is wonderful that we in the United States can freely believe in any god or gods we choose without government discrimination. As most Americans do, I feel strongly about preserving our freedom of religion as well as freedom from religion. Overall, most moderate believers are not the problem, and if they will work to modernize their own faith so that it can respect and accept the coexistence of other faiths (and no faith), it would be a wonderful thing for all of us. I think education is the only chance we have for this kind of modernization, but as a society, we can not be truly educated if it is taboo to learn about and talk about religion.

The absence of instruction about the world views of various religions is not "balance" and does not serve our youth. Craig Rusbult, a writer of Worldview Balance in Public Education, states,

> *"Effective teaching depends on the integrity and skill of teachers who think carefully, with wisdom and courage, about desirable goals; who build a solid foundation by adequate preparation and planning; and carry out their plans with sensitivity and respect."*

Creating a curriculum of balanced objectivity and neutrality is the responsibility of a public educator. It is legal, it is essential for the education of our youth, and it is vital for the betterment of our country. Obviously, it is not an easy task; emotions, personal beliefs, and public opinion make what is already a difficult, under-paid career even harder.

One of the things we can all do is actively promote public education that strives to present impartiality and objectivity about religions in our schools. Rusbult further says,

> *Teachers face tough choices and a dilemma. If a teacher ignores theistic perspectives, asymmetry and implications will produce a result that is not neutral. But if a teacher tries to introduce balance by discussing religion — even if this is done rationally with good taste and wisdom with an intention to educate rather than persuade — he can get in trouble. There is a reasonable fear, based on many actual cases, that this teacher will be inviting trouble in the form of complaints by parents, criticism by fellow teachers, pressure by administrators, and even lawsuits by 'separation of church and state' zealots.*

It is important that teachers not take advantage of their positions of authority and the vulnerability of the minds of young students. Neutrality, information, and objective content, while being sensitive to the importance of covering this topic, is what we all need to encourage and support as parents and tax payers.

Why not choose suicide?

If someone believes that when he dies he will go to a wonderful place that is much better than this earthly existence, why doesn't he just go?

Like the country song says, *"Everyone wants to go to heaven, just nobody wants to go tonight."* Obviously some do; we call them terrorists or victims of some insane cult leader when they blow themselves up or drink poison and die on command of their leader. So, why is it not more common that the normal believer in a glorious afterlife simply takes his own life and goes on to his reward? One answer is that each of the major religions considers suicide a serious sin and forbids it.

For example, the tenants of Judaism generally consider it a criminal act to commit suicide; someone who commits suicide is considered a murderer. This usually comes under the sixth commandment "Thou shalt not kill," but is killing oneself the same as killing others? The late Rabbi, Dr. Louis Jacobs, said, "There is, in fact, no direct prohibition of suicide in the Bible." In the Talmud (Bava Kama 91b), however, the prohibition is arrived at by a process of interpretation of the verse,

> *"and surely your blood of your lives will I require"* (Genesis 9: 5), *interpreted as: "I will require your blood if you yourselves*

> *shed it." It is possible that there is no direct*
> *prohibition of suicide because very few*
> *people of sound mind would be inclined to*
> *commit suicide in any event."*

Suicide, when it can be considered martyrdom, or when killing one's self to keep from being killed or tortured by the infidels, is usually considered acceptable in the Jewish faith.

The Catholic Encyclopedia describes suicide as a grave sin against god. It is intriguing to note that suicide is never condemned in the Bible. It was only declared a sin by St. Augustine in the fifth century. Yet most protestant Christians generally believe and express in public statements that euthanasia, even under extreme medical circumstances, is a serious sin as it keeps the person's soul out of heaven. Buddhists and Hindus generally consider suicide as the taking of a life, which is a major prohibition under any circumstance. The one exception for Buddhists is for those on the last leg of their reincarnation journey. In this exalted position, there is no future life on earth to be affected, and it does not seem to be an error to choose to move on to their reward.

Islam also views suicide as one of the greatest sins. The Qur'an states, *"And do not kill yourselves, surely God is most Merciful to you* (4:29)." Most members of Islam agree with this and state that one's life is not their own to take. Nevertheless, we've had a substantial increase in religion-related terrorist suicide bombings. From 1983 to 2000 there were 142 such attacks world-wide. From 2001 to 2003 there were 312, and in 2005 after the U.S. invasion of Iraq there were over 500. In all cases, over 70 percent of them were committed by religious groups.

Ginges, Hansen and Norenzayan, in a four-part study in the journal Psychological Science, reported that religious devotion, as indicated by frequency of prayer, was not found to be related to support of suicide attacks. Yet it was also found that mosque participation is strongly related to support of suicide attacks. They conclude that devotion alone does not increase one's propensity to commit suicide in order to kill others. Rather, this tendency is more related to the connection with the "in-group" that fosters this hate. I suspect this is true. Those who pray alone are likely to be more interested in their own salvation and are not interested in killing themselves or others.

The problem of people killing others, as well as killing themselves, is not related to merely believing in and praying to a supernatural god; the problem comes when the structure and process of a religion fosters hate and promotes the destruction of others who believe differently. Those young people with bombs strapped to their bodies are the victims of an organized social structure called Islam. It is the same with all the monotheistic religions, the anger-filled, hateful teaching by ministers, priests, rabbis and imams; they use their own followers as weapons to carry out their scriptures of hate.

As a nonbeliever, I'm still left with this puzzlement: If the after-life is believed to be so great, and a Christian genuinely believes they are going to such a place, prevented from going now only because of a decision made by St. Augustine centuries ago, why is that binding? Why don't they go now? Hundreds of believers in Islam blow themselves up while killing infidels, believing they get a "fast track" trip to a glorious place. And also note, the Christian Bible does not specifically forbid suicide for Christians. Why don't more of the faithful choose to go on to the next life now, especially if they are not having such a good time on this earth? Would it not make sense for unhappy people who believe in a glorious heaven and who believe that god will forgive them for being weak and desperately wanting to be with him, just go?

It is interesting to note that, in 2006, the overall rate of successful suicide was 10.9 deaths per 100,000 people. According to the US National Institute of Mental Health, the greatest indicators for suicide are depression and mental illness; religious devotion was not even mentioned as an indicator. Maybe the faithful have more than a little doubt about whether there actually is an afterlife, or at least they are uncertain about their getting in.

Have you ever been to a religious-based funeral service where the minister or religious leader says, "Don't be sad because the person is in a better place now"? I have heard this general statement many times, and it always makes me wonder why they had to suffer with illness, pain and misery if dying took them to a better place. A neighbor of mine recently told me that a hospitalized close, life-long friend had gone into a coma, so he called the hospital and asked the nurse to put the phone next to his ear. He then told his friend who he was, and then proceeded to yell, "DIE YOU OLD FART, JUST LET GO AND GO AHEAD AND DIE." He then hung up, saying that that was the most loving thing he could do to help his friend. I now think that my neighbor genuinely believed his friend would be better off dead, rather than continuing to "live" in a coma.

Does it seem right that all major monotheistic religions forbid medically-assisted suicide even when the patient has no hope of recovering, is in terrible pain, and wishes to die? I would think that the belief in a better place after death would encourage such medically-assisted suicides, but it seems to be just the opposite; all the fundamentalist faiths strongly fight against such action. I wonder if these believers actually do care more about some religious dogma than they do about the comfort of their loved ones. I sure hope my wife and children care more about me than some book and will "pull the plug" as soon as the quality of life tips permanently to the negative.

Who owns morals?

Many months ago, someone close to me suggested that, because I did not have a religious faith or did not subscribe to Christian scriptures, I would not be able to make moral decisions; I would, in essence, be a bad person. This truly bothered me. I have always considered myself a good person. I care about others. I do what I can to help those who are suffering, and I do not steal, lie, or cheat on my taxes. In short, I am a good, moral person.

My father, who I considered a kind, moral man, told me, *"Have all the fun you can have, and don't hurt anyone."* I also took that to mean to help everyone I can, which is what I try to do while I'm having all the fun I can. After all this research on religion, I'm now comfortable with my ethical values and my morals. I have a better feel for where they come from and why I observe them. Overall, I'm no longer bothered that someone might think, because I do not believe in Christian scriptures or their Christian God, that my morals are compromised; I now know that religion and scriptures have nothing to do with ethical values or morals. Here is why.

Morality and ethics are situational and relative. What is moral in one situation or society may not be in another. By moral, we usually mean things that are right and good to do, say, or think in a particular culture -- in short, what is acceptable. Morality does not inherently exist without defining what kind of morality we are talking about.

American morality, Christian morality, Islamic morality and South Chicago street gang morality are all different. What they have in common is that they are the accepted norms of conduct by members of that group in that culture. It is a way of acting that the group accepts as appropriate and expected to be part of the group. It can be called a "social interaction code." We learn this code as we learn our culture and as we learn how to behave in our culture.

Humans are not unique in having morals. Compared to other animals, we just have more of them, and more complex ones, just like we have more complex languages, social orders, and other specialized, uniquely human abilities. We need these social norms more than other animals because most animals have something we've lost, which is primarily a sense of instinct that directs much of their behaviors. Most primates, and many other animals as well, have a well-developed code of rights and wrongs that are learned and enforced in their social structure. They act in ways beneficial to the group that reflect moral decisions of kindness, care and social benefit, and they do it without our sense of religion.

Many people, both religious and nonreligious, believe that there is another way to describe moral behavior, and it involves innately "right" things to do as humans living on this planet. Such a universal morality might even now exist, and if it does not yet, as cultures blend into a more interdependent global society, it likely will exist some day. I would like to think there is an overarching and foundational human moral interaction code upon which we could all agree; I like the idea of Santa Clause, too.

When my religious friends talk about morals, I believe they actually mean "Christian" morals. For a moment, I will give them the benefit of the doubt that they are meaning a set of comprehensive "correct" ways of being that is "right" for all humans. A few communities have legal rules of conduct that approximate what I would like to see as universal behaviors, but then I realize that they are just my ideas of right and wrong and are not necessarily universal. What does seem to be universal is that everyone wants to be treated fairly and with an appreciation as an individual worthy of respect. The "Golden Rule" goes a long way to describe what might become universal moral behavior. I have had trouble finding a religious listing of "human morals" because most holy books that I have looked at include hate, child abuse, sexual abuse, slavery, murder, and torture of humans as normal, acceptable behavior. I personally have a problem including any of this as acceptable, moral behavior that will work in our future global community.

Most religions have rules, commandments, or even laws, but mostly they are just common sense guidelines that exist almost everywhere. So where does "religion" get off claiming ownership as the only source of moral development of society?

Actually, I think most people have it backwards; they think religion is the source of their codes of social conduct. In fact, it is the people of each culture who develop their own moral codes, and it is the religious orthodoxy, also created by human culture, which monitors and enforces their codes of societal conduct. All cultures have rules of moral behavior, even those with unusually little religious participation. What religion seems to bring to the table is greater motivation for enforcement than is provided by a secular system, namely the promise of salvation. For the faithful, the controlling principle is that if one breaks the moral code, he will have to repeat his life as a lower animal in the next reincarnation, or alternatively, he will burn in hell for all eternity. This is why some think that those of us without a religiously-based "fear of God" are running around totally out of control because we are not afraid of the consequences. It is not like that at all. The actual consequences of breaking moral codes are the same for everyone -- societal disgrace, loss of respect, punishment for violation of secular laws, etc. Most atheists, or discredists, just like most religious people, are moral people. We do the right thing because we think it makes sense (and there are likely laws against doing bad things with serious consequences.)

I have read several books about this subject, and they seem to make it immensely complicated. Perhaps it is, but, for me, it is more like my sex drive -- simply natural. For example, evolutionarily speaking, men are attracted to women sexually for the procreation of children (unless they are gay and then to the same sex, for other reasons). We have this sex drive primarily to continue our species, the same as any other animal. But if we are only attracted to each other to have children, why would a man be attracted to a woman he knows is on the pill, or after he has had a vasectomy? Because it is a normal, natural drive and does not go away, even though we find ways to short circuit the original planned outcome.

It is the same with moral behavior. Most people are just naturally moral; we want to help an injured bird, a hurt puppy, or a starving child. We want to be good. It makes sense that, in the arc of human development, we have learned to be kind and caring. Being good and kind makes sense for the successful continuation of the species. Even though we may short circuit this tendency from time to time with hate and violence, the human animal has developed a natural inclination to do the right thing toward other living things. Humans are not born evil or sinful, and we don't need a religion, or anyone to die for us, or any list of commandments, to make us moral. In fact, there is continuing and fascinating research showing the inherent psychological rewards of experiencing human empathy toward others leading to what we'd call moral behavior.

To be sure, in order to be able to act in moral ways, people need to have first met primary, basic needs of survival, such as food, shelter, etc. We are, first of all, animals trying to survive. Once these individual primary needs are met, we have the natural inclination to be good, moral people. The psychologist Abraham Maslow first introduced this concept as a hierarchy of needs in 1943. The most basic levels are physiological and security needs, such as water, air, food, and sleep, followed by needs of safety and security. The third level, the social needs, includes morality and functioning in a social group. It is also true that there are a very few people who are truly evil; mental illness and psychotic behavior does occur, but it exists within religious followers as well as among nonreligious people. Religion, or lack of it, is not an indicator of such behavior.

Belonging to a monotheistic religion has not seemed to increase moral behavior. If I were a member of one of these faiths, I think I would be embarrassed about the history of my faith, and I would not try to sell it as being more moral than not believing. I won't belabor listing all the atrocities that have been done to human beings in the name of religion; we are all familiar with the religious wars leading to genocide and the burning of thousands of innocent women as witches. There were also the inquisitions where, in the Spanish Inquisition alone, for example, over 2,000 heretics were burned at the cross. Consider the more recent incidents of child abuse by Catholic priests, the frequent scandals regarding infidelity in Christian ministry, and the massive gender-abuse practiced by millions of male Muslims. These are the outcomes of following the holy scriptures of these great religions.

Here's what I mean. Consider these scripture-based statements about how to treat others having a different belief:

". . . boiling water shall be poured over their heads, which shall melt what is their bellies and their skins as well, and for them are whips of iron, and whenever want to leave, from grief, they shall be turned back, and hate the chastisement of burning." (Qur'ân 2.85, 22.19-22)

". . . show them no pity. Do not spare them or protect them. You must surely put them to death. Stone him to death who tries to turn you away from the lord your God." (Jehovah – Deuteronomy 13:8-10)

". . . if anyone comes to me and does not hate his father and mother, his wife and children, his brother and sisters – yes, even his own life – he cannot be my disciple. . . . This is how it will be in the end: the angels will come and separate the wicked from the righteous and throw them into the fiery furnace, where you will weep and gnash your teeth." (Jesus Christ - Matthew 13:49-50, Luke 14:26)

". . . and all those who preach false doctrines, and all those who commit whoredoms, and pervert the right way of the Lord, wo, wo, wo be unto them, saith the Lord God Almighty, for

they shall be thrust down to hell!" (Book of Mormon – 2nd Nephi 28:15)

Religion's claim to having ownership of "morality" is just a red herring, an empty claim that has no substance. Millions of people behave in moral ways without religion. If we can get to an accepted and enacted universal code of moral behavior one day, it will be the result of natural inclination and desire of all healthy humans, once their basic survival needs have been met, to be kind to people, to take care of all living things, and to treat others as they would like to be treated. Being moral has nothing to do with religion!

What is spirituality?

Can a person not believe in a supernatural god and still be spiritual? It all depends on what one means by spiritual. The Dalai Lama says:

> *"I believe an important distinction can be made between religion and spirituality. Religion I take to be concerned with faith in the claims to salvation of one faith tradition or another. Spirituality I take to be concerned with qualities of the human spirit -- love and compassion, patience, tolerance, forgiveness, contentment, a sense of responsibility, a sense of harmony -- that bring happiness both to self and others."*

Here is how Daniel Dennett defines spirituality:

> *"If you can approach the world's complexities, both its glories and its horrors, with an attitude of humble curiosity, acknowledging that however deeply you have seen, you have only just scratched the surface; you will find worlds within worlds, beauties you could not heretofore imagine, and your own mundane preoccupations will shrink to proper size, not all that important in the greater scheme of things. Keeping ready at hand that awestruck vision of the world while dealing with the demands of daily living is no easy exercise, but it is definitely worth the effort; if you can stay centered and engaged, you will find the hard choices easier, the right words*

will come to you when you need them, and you will indeed be a better person. That, I propose, is the secret to spirituality, and it has nothing at all to do with believing in an immortal soul, or in anything supernatural."

Personally, I like the "awe" factor that I feel under a clear, starry night or when I watch a beautiful sunset. I feel connected to an amazing, extraordinary, and beautiful universe. I have the delightful opportunity to live in the Northwest part of our country. When I stand on a mountain glacier and look across these beautiful mountain tops, or gaze at a glorious sunset, it is hard to imagine that this is anything but a spiritual experience. To watch a killer whale splash and put on a show in the wild or to smell the fresh, salt air on a warm summer day -- that is spiritual. For me, it is being connected to the earth, to all living things, being directly related to other animals, and in balance with all of it -- that is my version of spirituality.

Most of us also do not want to miss out on what our culture has determined to be "good" spirituality, such as having team spirit or being a person with a "good spirit." I do not clearly know what people mean by such a statement as, "he has a good spirit," but I know that it is good to have one. So I try to keep my spirit up, whatever that means.

Recently, it has become popular in America to diminish the stature of religion, as various religious groups and behaviors have received a lot of negative publicity. Their ritual and dogmatic connotations have become suspect and unpopular, and it is now more common for people to say they are spiritual but not religious. A study in 2009 found 24 percent of the people surveyed stating that they were not religious, but they considered themselves to be spiritual; nevertheless, 69 percent of this same group said they believe in a god. It all seems just semantic to me; if you believe in something supernatural you are likely religious. If you mean that spirituality is an internal mental force of awe, wonder and appreciation for what is, of amazement about what exists in all its wonder, then you can be spiritual without religion. Yet, if you consider the root word "spirit" in spirituality and actually believe in an external, supernatural force yet undiscovered by our current science, such as a ghost, it sounds a lot like religion to me.

Religion involves the basic human need to believe in something supernatural -- call it a god, a dead ancestor, or a spirit guide. It is all about something greater than oneself, something that interacts with us in some nonphysical way. Perhaps the majority of people are religious because they are inherently afraid of their own mortality, and they need answers as to why they exist. It seems that the need to be protected by something, to be "saved," is always a crucial part of being religious. For the most part, these are external, supernatural answers that have been created for thousands of years by man to answer some of the big, and so far, unanswerable questions of life.

Thankfully, nothing is forever. If there were no end to our lifespan and life just went on forever, what would be the awe in seeing another beautiful sunset? There would be no limit, and even sunsets would get boring. We can be reflective and appreciative -- spiritual -- about just "what is," about loving and living, especially knowing that one day it will end. I do not look forward to my life ending, but I don't fear it; I don't need to be saved. I just want to live every day that I do have with awe. What I leave behind are my children, grandchildren and the memories of those who have known me, and this will be more than enough. The need for salvation, so essential to Christians, seems to imply that we need to be saved from life. Yet for many of us, life is wonderful – full of wonder -- because it is so fleeting, and that is spiritual.

Can scientists be religious?

Can a person be a scientist, or even merely agree that evolution is true, and still believe in god? Kenneth Miller, author of Finding Darwin's God, thinks so. In fact, he is a scientist and a leading defender of Darwin's brilliant discovery. He agrees that it is one of the greatest truths in science today, and yet he believes in the Christian God. He admits he is among a very small minority of scientists who do, but he argues that science and religion should not be in conflict because they deal with entirely different domains. He agrees with Steven Jay Gould who has said, "*The lack of conflict between science and religion arises from a lack of overlap between their respective domains of professional expertise --science in the empirical constitution of the universe, and religion in the search for proper ethical values and the spiritual meaning of our lives.*"

Yet, Gould is also seen as one of the greatest threats to creationism and is anything but a friend to traditional religion. Gould has clearly postulated in his book, Wonderful Life, that if the evolutionary clock were rewound a million times or more, the universe would never end up with humans again. This is the nature of random variation and one of the great strengths of evolution itself. According to Miller, the reality of evolution and of all modern science is not a threat to creationism. He, as a scientist, sees the beauty of evolution as reinforcement to the intricacy and depth of his god

Questions About Religion 81

as the master designer who used natural selection, biology, and physics to play out his plan.

This interpretation of god as a designer of the universe is not new, but what Miller brings to the argument is that he thinks there are two holes in the materialism of science that support his position and makes it a sound argument. The first is the science of the exceptionally small -- quantum theory -- with its random, unpredictable component. Basically, what quantum physicists have found is that there is a small percentage of particle behavior that is always random, or at least does not conform to the currently known laws; such behavior is called quantum indeterminacy. This is well explained by Stephen Hawking in The Universe in a Nutshell, although he still leaves me confused, as I'm sure most non-scientific types like me are. But, I do get the idea that it just happens, and that scientists adjust for it in quantum research through averaging and other complex mathematical techniques.

The other hole in science that Miller sees is the very "large" -- it is just too amazing, too unlikely, to him that the fundamental forces in the universe are just exactly as they need to be for the universe, and for us, to exist. These forces include the absolute value of gravity ('g'), the strong nuclear force, electromagnetism, and the resonance level of atoms, which all have to be exactly as they are for the universe to work. If everything is just random chance, as science says it is, there is no way this could happen, he says. Therefore, the quantum randomness and the alignment of these other forces (called the Anthropic Principle) gives him an explanation for believing in and explaining the cleverness of the designer.

Well maybe so; I sure don't know. Most scientists are quite willing to say they don't know everything and likely never will. Even the things we think we know can, and do, turn out to be wrong. When I read the new theories of physics, they are mind-boggling, to say the least. And these are exceedingly smart people who come up with these wild and crazy theories that actually explain how the universe works. As wild as they seem, multiple universes and vibrating string theories have mathematical evidence to support them. I'm sure more will be learned and explained in the future. What all this has to do with this discussion is to say that religion is only one way of explaining how the universe got the way it is, and it has no evidence to support it. Natural science, on the other hand, goes a long way in explaining the natural world and how it got this way, and scientists have a lot of evidence that they are right, even if they do not have all the answers.

Of course, Daniel Dennett and Dawkins and the other atheists writing about this Anthropic Principle have a lot to say. In short, as I understand them, they say that, as Hawking and other physicists explain it, we are just looking backwards, and like any evolutionary observation, it had to be that way for us even to be here to look. They site that there may have been multiple big bangs that started this all, or maybe there are no other options for these constants, or we might be in a loop of collapsing universes, or perhaps there are an infinite number of multiple universes and we are in the one that got it right. All of these possibilities are just as likely, if not more so, as the notion that a god made it the way it is, just so we could come along billions and billions of years later and serve him.

What all this means to me is that if a scientist determines there to be a hole in what science explains that cannot (yet) be answered, it is not a deal-breaker for the validity of the scientific process, because science does not know everything and likely never will. What I read between the lines in Miller's book is that he is looking for an answer to the big question of "why." For him, finding a god gives him a purpose, a reason to exist.

"Purpose for the existence of man . . ." I have heard this statement many times, and I admit I have never understood it until reading Miller's book. I now believe that when people are brought up with and indoctrinated into a religious belief system, they gain great comfort from thinking that their lives and all human lives have a divinely inspired purpose. They are taught that they are part of something wonderful, and their social structure reinforces this with the comfort of belonging. Who knows? Maybe finding a scientific method for justifying a god does give purpose. I'm rather embarrassed to say that I have never thought about it before; a "greater purpose" has never even entered my mind. For Miller, and for many smart people, even when they strip away all the dogma, superstitions, and stories, and when they can see that science is not their enemy and that evolution is as true as gravity, they still need to have a purpose, some reason to be alive. A god can give them this comfort. As Miller does, they can find a logical flaw in contemporary science; they compartmentalize their belief in a god as being in the domain of spiritualism, and they leave science in the domain of materialism.

Let me digress a minute. I find myself fascinated with this idea of needing a reason to exist, a purpose to my life -- something bigger than myself. It sounds like a good idea to hold that reasoning. So what could it be? If everything happens merely by chance, which I think is the case, and as Gould says, rewinding the evolutionary clock would produce something totally different every time, what purpose could my little life have on this little rock in a little solar system in a little galaxy in one of what may be an infinite number of universes? The other day a doe with a couple of young deer walked through our yard. The mamma deer was clearly teaching her children how good my wife's roses were to eat. I wondered what the greater purpose was for this lovely doe. Does she serve a bigger purpose? Well, I think she served a perfect purpose. She brought her young into the world, she lived as part of her natural community, and she will die at some point, with her decaying body providing nourishment to animals and vegetation, and thus fulfill her role. Why should there be more than that for any living thing?

As humans, we can have a greater role to play, our community can be much larger, and we can have a positive impact in a much bigger way than we usually do. But day-to-day, we simply bring our young into the world, try our best to teach them how to be successful happy people, and we live our life trying to have a positive impact on and in our community. Because of our larger brain and our ability to control our environment, our community can be very big; I feel mine is the whole world. I want to contribute to that world the best I can, leave my genes through my children, and leave a positive impact on this world. That is my purpose, it is plenty big, and I feel just fine about it. Gee, now that I got that out, I guess I can now die.

Back to science and religion . . . A belief in a God, as Kenneth Miller has said, is not the problem. He states that the Bible should not be taken literally, that the stories were written that way because that is the way people were, and that is what they understood at the time. Again, a belief in a supernatural god that gives comfort and is humane and rational towards others and towards our planet is not the problem. Science has broken down most all of the superstitions and made all the stories just stories. We now know that demons don't cause illness, virgins don't have babies, and horses don't fly to heaven. On the other hand, science does not and can not disprove that there is a god. God could have started it all, planning, for example, for a sentient creature to crawl out of the ocean at some point, and evolution was just one of his tools. No one can know if a god does or does not exist; people can believe that there is or that there is not a god, but there is no proof.   Science does not disprove the existence of a god, it only explains the real world. People like Miller, who sees science and evolution as just part of god's great plan, can decide to move their comfort with and need for a god into another domain and not try to make it fit into the rules of science. The world would be a much better place if all monotheistic believers could do this and if all of the angry atheists could have tolerance with such a positive and adaptive belief. The problem is that many people are stuck, believing literally in a two thousand year old book that teaches hatred, abuse and violence.

Part Three - - The Big Problems With Religion

Is believing in god a problem?

No, the problem is not that people believe in a god; for the most part, it is wonderful that we live in a country where we are all free to believe in anything we want. It is perfectly okay to believe in and pray to an invisible god if a person wants to, and to develop a church full of followers to do the same. Where the problem lies is when members of any faith believe that their faith gives justification for them to do harm to others who believe differently. In short, the problem is not in believing; it is when the structures, rules, scriptures and dogmas of a faith require or encourage members of a faith to do harm against others who believe differently.

This is a really big problem, because half the world now believes in one of the three major monotheistic religions -- Christianity, Islam, or Judaism -- which are all based upon the same basic foundation, that of a jealous and war-oriented God. All three trace their roots back to Abraham and have used the Old Testament or the Torah as the foundation of their faith. They all came out of the same small area of the desert where war, slavery, and abuse to women and children were the way of life.

Millions of people get comfort and happiness from believing in a god. I see no problem with this, in and of itself. Survival and finding happiness in this world is hard. If a belief in a god and quiet talks with oneself in prayer help some people feel good, so much the better. I want to be very clear about this. The problem is believing that these holy books, written nearly two thousand years ago in a time of perpetual war when slavery was the norm, abuse of women and children was accepted, and superstition of all types was practiced everywhere, should be taken as the foundation of how we should live today. THAT is the problem.

The authors of these books were merely mortal men who thought the world was flat, that the universe rotated around the earth, and that demons caused illness. Why would we now want to adopt their words as the way we should treat each other, form governments, decide who gets what medicine, or decide what is moral? For example, the Bible is clear that it is the duty of every believer to kill gay men. If a man lies with a male as with a woman, both of them have committed an abomination; they shall be put to death (Leviticus 20:13). What does this kind of instruction do to people who believe this as the foundation of their faith? Thankfully, few practice this today, but it is easy to see how such prejudice affects our society.

If you were to go to any major book store and browse the books shelved under "philosophy," you could pick almost any modern book to read, and it would be a better guide on how to live today than the Torah, the Bible, or the Qur'an. Walk through any major grocery store, and there you will find a dozen, good self-help books that will teach you how to improve your life. None of these secular books will tell you it is your duty to kill people who believe in a different god, or that it is acceptable to own slaves, or to abuse women as inferior people. We have moved beyond such ideas; the age of enlightenment arrived long ago. In short, these holy books being the foundations of the major religions of the world today are the problem. There is nothing magical in them. They were all written in a time of ignorance about our world today, and they all foster violence, cruelty, and hate.

I don't dislike learning history. In fact, I think it is wonderful; the written works of antiquity are amazing. We should all learn from these great authors of the past. In fact, there is much to learn from the religious books that are held to be holy. I don't want them to go away; they contain so many good things that are worth learning. When I go to a bookstore or a library and browse the philosophy section, I find many great classics I very much want to read. I often try to put myself in the time of these great authors and think how amazing it was that they had the ideas and thoughts about which they wrote. However, when we uncritically accept that their ideas are all literally true and that they are the guidebooks for our lives, in all ways for all times, we are in trouble.

Faith -- belief in a supernatural god or a spirit -- is natural, and, in and of itself, is neither right nor wrong. People who believe in such things are no better or no worse than those who do not. It does not even matter what a person believes. What matters is how that person interacts with the world and others in it. Any faith system which uses documents as a guide to one's life today that are from a time of immense struggle and of great ignorance, even with moderation and a lot of interpretation, are relying on material that does not fit today's world. Reliance on old scriptures as the word of each of their gods is what holds the monotheistic desert religions in the frozen hatred and violence that we live with today.

Why can't religions get along?

So, why can't these big three religions just coexist peacefully if they are so similar? It is because they all actively promote the destruction of people who do not believe exactly as they do. The very nature of a religion based on a monotheistic, jealous god is that it is the only true and right faith. Therefore, if any one of them is correct and true, the others have to be wrong and false. All three are based upon the premise that their adherents have the right and duty to kill all who do not believe as they do because theirs is the one and only true faith. In short, this is the difference between modern western religions (monotheistic) and the polytheistic and animistic religions of the past. When people believed that there can be more than one god, such as in the Parthenon systems of Greece and ancient Rome, they didn't need to kill each other over which god the people prayed to. True, they killed each other over a lot of other things, but when one faith claimed to have the God of the "chosen people" and to be the only true god, it could not just take its place as another statue in the building and be worshipped with all the rest. Holy wars, abuse of women and children, and hatred toward all others have been the result ever since, all resulting from the influence of these three monotheistic faiths. In the world today, we are still hating and killing because the infidels (all who "don't believe as I do") believe in the wrong god. This is a mighty big problem. The attacks on the World Trade Center and other places in the U.S. on "9/11" are just one example of how large a problem it is. Now we are faced with entire countries that are under the control of religious leaders who believe they have the right and duty to kill and either now have, or will soon have, nuclear weapons to use against the infidels.

It is not an exaggeration to say that we now face the greatest danger to the continuation of the human species that has ever existed.

The threat is no longer just a small group of exiles from Egypt slaughtering small villages of "other" people. If Iran or Pakistan bombs Israel and then Israel retaliates, it could well be over for all human life on this planet. While some fundamentalist believers may think this is just the revelation upon which we have been waiting, for the vast majority of humanity it will be the ultimate end. The bottom line: the human species evolved, took control of the planet, and then destroyed itself. In the big picture of earth's time, this will just be a minor event; life will continue, and maybe even intelligent life will crawl out of the oceans the next time.

Yet, we are told every day by our media and our politically correct, "polite" society that we should not talk about, and especially not challenge, religion; it is not "proper" or "respectful." Will it be appropriate to talk about it when one of these fundamentalist religious leaders decides it is right and proper to launch a nuclear missile at a country where those people believe differently? This becomes quite likely when, as is the case in all three major faiths, the attacking leaders believe that, if they die while killing others who believe differently, they will reap the benefits of their particular version of heaven, and it will be glorious. Again, the problem is not that, as human animals, we are pre-programmed to believe in supernatural agents; the significant problem is when the human leaders of the religions associated with those agents call for the destruction of all who think and believe differently.

"And whoever flies in Allah's way, he will find in the earth many a place of refuge and abundant resources; and whoever goes forth from his house flying to Allah and His Apostle, and then death overtakes him, his reward is indeed with Allah and Allah is Forgiving, Merciful." (Qur'an, 4-100)

". . . that certain base fellows have gone out among you and have drawn away the inhabitants of the city saying, 'Let us go and serve other gods which you have not known, then you shall inquire and make search and ask diligently; and behold, if it be true and certain that such an abominable thing has been done among you, you shall surely put the inhabitants of that city to the sword, destroying it utterly, all who are in it and its cattle, with edge of the sword.' " (Deuteronomy 13:13-15)

It is the hate and jealousy that exists within the scriptures of the major monotheistic religions that is the big problem with religion. For the most part, all three monotheistic religions have no tolerance for those who believe in a different god or for those who do not believe in any supernatural god. One can find historical examples of competition among the "eastern" religions, even leading to wars, but for the most part, they have found ways to live and let live. The Buddhists, for example, are far more interested in improving their own lives and searching for inner perfection than in outward war against others. By contrast, the western "desert" religions have always fostered hatred, brutality, and genocide towards those who do not believe the same as they do. The history of the last two thousand years makes it clear -- without radical changes in how these three monotheistic faiths function, we are in for some big problems. The moderates, especially in the Christian faith, will say I'm over reacting and that they don't actually act this way. True, the followers of Abraham are now, for the most part, much more subtle than in the days of Joshua, where women and children were killed by the thousands for living in the wrong place, but the same scriptures still guide the same followers!

That portion of the modern brain that does not bother to question the logic of one's faith is still making decisions based upon a 1600 to 2000 year-old book, a collection of writings about a bunch of tribes competing for limited resources in a cruel and desperate time. Surely we can find something more relevant to our current lives and more humanitarian on which to base our need for a supernatural god.

It is time to modernize these monotheistic religions. Until last year, it was the US policy to deprive the infidels of AIDS medication if they mentioned the word abortion in their clinics. We still bomb civilians and take over another country because we think they are "agents of evil." After all, they believe differently than we do so it does not matter that we are killing them, and for the most part we Christians think they deserve to die. Just listen to Christian talk radio if you doubt this. Good people need to say no to religious-based hate.

Even moderates within all three faiths are influenced by their scriptures about war, jealousy, and a single "right way" for all time and in all situations. These documents do affect their followers in subtle ways that may not seem too harmful, but ultimately they lead to unacceptable discrimination, bigotry and, finally, hatred. People have opinions and make decisions based upon what they have personally learned, experienced, reasoned, or believe, and people do believe what is written in their holy books.

The modern world has advanced on many fronts. Our technology is amazing, and our physical and natural sciences are mind-boggling. Politically, we have learned a lot about managing large populations. But where faith is concerned, we are stuck 2000 years in the past. What this limitation of spiritual growth and development has done is to perpetuate the prejudices and the ways of people from the past. Where the beliefs of the past were obviously wrong, such as thinking the earth was the center of the universe, we have recognized the error and moved on. Where ancient peoples wrote down their prejudices, such as their social norms of slavery and abuse as religious doctrine and scripture, we are still stuck with them as the "right and only way" and never-changing. These old messages have an impact on modern culture; the majority of people report that they believe it as "gospel." The Bible, as a foundational book on which to base one's values and daily decisions, leads to subtle prejudices and intolerance, even in those who overlook the obvious violence and hatred.

The Qur'an is similar in its lack of toleration. *"So when the sacred months have passed away, then slay the idolaters wherever you find them, and take them captives and besiege them and lie in wait for them in every ambush."* (Qur'an, 9:5) What is especially scary about this is the way the followers of the Islamic faith, which is commonly thought to be the fastest growing religion, believe their holy book in a totally literal way. To a Muslim, the Qur'an is the literal word of Allah, and there is no room to accept it as merely guidelines or as metaphor; it is all to be taken literally. The west is seen as evil, and it is the responsibility of all devout Muslims to fight against this perceived evil. *"O you who believe! Fight those of the unbelievers who are near to you and let them find in you hardness; and know that Allah is with those who guard against evil."* (Qur'an, 9:123)

In addition, most Islamic countries operate their governments based first upon their faith, and at a distant second, upon secular logic. If you live in one of many Islamic countries, the laws of Islam, called Sharia, are first and foremost the laws that the government enforces. True, it is the Islamic extremist that we credit today for the current wave of terrorism. But the premise is clear -- Islam, similar to the Judeo-Christian faiths, is based upon no toleration for anyone who believes differently than they do.

Nonie Darwish, writing in her book, Cruel and Usual Punishment, says

"However, let me be clear: The West must understand that the problem is not individual Muslims as much as it is Muslim scriptures commanding them to kill. The question is, 'What will the West do to protect its citizens from violent commandments against non-Muslims that appear in the Qur'an, Hadith, and Sharia?' "

In all societies, social order is controlled by a secular set of laws or religious rules of conduct (commandments), or both. Thousands of years ago, as societies grew in population, it was far more practical to control large areas and numbers of people by religious rules than with soldiers. Under religion, there is a "watchman" or god that is seeing everything that people do, and this method of control costs remarkably little for the rulers to maintain.

Our history is full of partnerships between kings and priests to maintain control of the masses. In addition, governments have used religion to increase their effectiveness in both defending their territory and expanding it. People are far more willing to die for a belief that insures them salvation than for a material reason. This has been especially true when merely staying alive was hard. At least with a faith that promised something better after death, they had something to look forward to, no matter how hard their life was on this earth. Therefore, the faiths that controlled the masses, defended the home land, and expanded the territory became the most successful. The outcome of this societal advantage is the primacy of the current major monotheistic, war-oriented religions.

The list of conflicts about religion is almost endless: the Spanish Inquisition; the Manichean Schism; the persecution of Huguenots; the fights between the Catholics and the Protestants, the Christians and the Muslims, the Hindus and the Muslims; and the more than six million Jews killed by Hitler's Third Reich. There seems to be no end to the violence people can do to each other under the name of religion.

The concepts of right, wrong, and truth have historically been claimed as the domain of religion. By contrast, in modern science and its scientific method, as well as in secular rules or laws, we find things to be mostly true or right until we learn more and change our minds. In "rational" life, we are always learning and advancing what we call facts and truths. We now know that the world is not flat, that a god in a chariot does not pull the sun across the sky, and that time is not the constant we thought it was. But in faith, things are very different.

The "Truth" found in faith is based upon a set of beliefs that are true and not to be questioned, tested or ever changed. In faith, a belief is what the person <u>wants</u> to be true. It may have nothing to do with "reality truth." Therefore, if a religion's version of truth is that their way is the only right way, and only their god can be right, all other "truths" claimed by other religions have to be wrong and false. This logic results in an outcome similar to the inter-tribal contacts of primitive man, where anthropologists note that when two clans of humans met for the first time, there were only two options -- join in a kinship as one group or kill each other.

Why all the violence in religions?

Violence is hard to describe because, like moral behavior, it is conditional. What some societies call acceptable behavior, other call unacceptable violence. A teacher hitting a student in a school setting used to be very common "discipline" in this country. The smack of a ruler across the knuckles or a good spanking by the vice principal was the norm. Today, most American parents would find this unacceptable violence. Another example is marital rape, which only recently came to be considered unacceptable violence in the United States; many cultures still don't even have such a concept. In some cultures and under some religions, even murdering your own daughter is acceptable and is called an honor killing. Wife-beating is common in much of the world. Body mutilation is accepted as normal, and many young girls go through a brutal genital mutilation that, to us, is abuse. Yet, the girls in some Moslem countries are often proud to be made "pure" in the eyes of their god.

Major examples of religious violence include holy wars where the reason for killing was strictly to expel or exterminate a group of people because they had the wrong religion. While this has been a prominent part of the history of many religions, it is seldom the sole reason today. Today, we see religion added to political, racial or ethnic conflicts. We see Sunnis fighting with Shiites about who now has power in Iraq. We see Jews fighting with Muslims about a strip of land that they both claim.

Hindus in India fight with Muslims about who has a right to govern areas of the country and which of them are the invaders. It seems that, when a religion's scripture says not only is violence justifiable, but mandated, religion is used as a justification for hatred when actually there are other cultural or social reasons for conflict. Religion, nevertheless, makes it easy for believers to act on their issues. In Christianity, it was the burning of thousands of women as witches and the confiscating of their possessions for the gain of the church that might be seen as the ultimate justification of violence by scripture. *"You shall not permit a sorceress to live."* (Exodus 22, 18). Such a statement is not just an old way of saying something; it is a "law" of religion, a rule to live by.

Violence against others who the scriptures say should be put to death is not just something out of our history books. On January 4, 2010, the Seattle Times ran a story on the front page about a "life-and-death gay-rights fight." It seems that three evangelical Christians (Lively, Brundidge, Schmierer) traveled to Uganda and lectured widely on the threat that homosexuals posed to Bible-based values. They lectured about how homosexual men often sodomize teenage boys and how "the gay movement is an evil institution." Following the conference, a Ugandan politician introduced the Anti-Homosexual Bill of 2009, which legalizes killing (by hanging) homosexuals. It seems that conservative Christians have enormous influence over the people and their political leaders in this predominantly rural country. Uganda is not alone in its human rights violence based upon scripture. Gay men can legally be stoned to death in northern Nigeria, "because," after all, the Bible says, *"If a man lies with a man as one lies with a woman, both of them have done what is detestable. They must be put to death; their blood will be on their own heads."* Leviticus 20:13

Christianity is not the only force to decree such violence towards homosexuals. The Moslem countries of Iran and Yemen have the death penalty for being found guilty of homosexuality, for after all, the Qur'an, similar to the Bible, says to put them to death.

"Of all the creatures in the world, will ye approach males, and leave those whom Allah has created for you to be your mates? Nay, ye are a people transgressing (all limits)! They said: 'If thou desist not, O Lut! Thou wilt assuredly be cast out!' He said: 'I do detest your doings:' 'O my Lord! Deliver me and my family from such things as they do!' So we delivered him and his family, - all except an old woman who lingered behind. But the rest we destroyed utterly. We rained down on them a shower (of brimstone): and evil was the shower on those who were admonished (but heeded not)! Verily in this is a Sign: but most of them do not believe. And verily thy Lord is He, the Exalted in Might, Most Merciful." (Qur'an 26:165-175)

Violence against consenting adults in the privacy of their own homes has been, until a recent Supreme Court decision overturning such laws, a criminal offense here in the United States. This was predominantly the case in the "bible belt," where states such as Oklahoma and Missouri have had laws against oral or anal sex by same-sex couples. Florida, Alabama, Louisiana, Mississippi North and South Carolina have had similar criminal laws for anyone who is found guilty of consensual sodomy. It is no accident that these states are strongly Christian fundamentalist.

Why is it so common to see so much violence fostered in religions? It all goes back to fear and intolerance. When a truth is believed by faith, there is no room for doubt or questioning. Under the rules of faith, only one set of truths can be correct, and all others have to be wrong. Because religious truths are not based upon rational reasoning, and therefore there is no need for evidence that they are correct, their holders have a universal fear of any challenge to those truths. This fear, like all fear, is able to be turned into anger, and then to hatred, and finally to violence. Perhaps this is too simple an explanation of all the hatred and violence that exists in people who are following their scriptures, but I think it is the same as that which we see in all people when they fear losing something very important; they are quick to turn to violence to preserve what is important to them.

Again, belief in a supernatural god, in an afterlife, and all the rest of the superstitions that go with these beliefs, are natural for humans to adopt. They feel good, they bring comfort to the believers, and those who believe do not want to lose them or have them threatened by others who have different beliefs. In addition, those with no supernatural beliefs also pose a threat. After all, if anyone else is correct, the believer must be wrong. It is easy to see just how scary this possibility must be. Again, fear goes to anger, which goes to violence.

The problem is not just violence; it is also subtle bigotry, psychological abuse, and a refusal to accept reason and progress in scientific information. When a religion teaches that only some are the "chosen ones" or that only a few who practice the "correct" religious procedures will achieve salvation and all others deserve to go to hell, it teaches bigotry. When a faith forces women to live as if they were inferior to men and not even worth being educated, it is abuse. When the holy scriptures collide with and overrule reason and accepted science and they prevent advancements that could benefit everyone, it sustains ignorance. For example, in 2007, during an American presidential debate, three candidates proudly raised their hands to declare that they did not believe in evolution. President George W. Bush said, "The jury is still out" on evolution. It has been over a hundred years since Darwin's death, and educated people all over the world accept evolution as scientific fact, but when it threatens religious scripture, the more fundamentalist-inclined faithful cannot allow reason to prevail.

Does anyone honestly believe that the earth is only six thousand years old, just because that is how the dates add up in the Bible? Can any reasonable person believe that all animal species were created at one time? Can anyone think that humans ran around avoiding the dinosaurs? We have plenty of evidence of the evolution of life on this planet, and yes, it was just a long series of small mutations or accidents that led to us being what we are today. As Stephen Jay Gould says in his must-read book, Wonderful Life, "If you rewound the evolutionary clock and did it all over again, it would work out totally different every time." We have learned a lot, but our major religions are literally prehistoric; they continue to teach ignorance, hate and violence.

Many writers today look down on belief in a god and feel that believing has to stop. I don't share that view because gods have never hurt anyone; it is the people following their religious rules that have hurt people. In short, we must ask if the scriptures of the current large, monotheistic religions are the problem, or if it is the belief in a single god that causes followers to do such damage to other people.

There are literally thousands of gods that are believed in today. If we include all the gods of the past which are not popular today, there are tens of thousands of gods. Gods come in all types. Most have human-like personalities; some are kind and loving; and others are jealous, cruel and warlike. The faithful that believe in these gods write books, mantras, or verses to describe their god and to tell future generations how to practice their faith. Each generation of followers uses these religious documents as its "instruction books," prescribing how to practice their faith and live their lives. Therefore, I can only conclude that it is the attachment to these books that keep a faith from evolving, from advancing, even as people learn new ways of solving problems or of staying healthy and happy. As I see it, it is the holy books that are the problem and will continue to be the problem as long as the faithful follow them as the ultimate word of their gods and refuse to update them as needed to keep up with the scientific and social advancements of humanity.

Looking at the Bible, for example, and just taking the first section (Genesis), I come away with many concerns that make this book seem to me the problem. For example, the creation story separates man (I don't mean humans) from all other living things and gives him dominion over everything. This seems to suggest that man is not part of all living things, that he is not interrelated with everything on this planet, but has the right to destroy because it was all made for him. Could this be part of the reason some believers of the Bible do not feel a responsibility to care for the environment? After all, Genesis tells them it was created just for their use.

What about sexism as described in this first section above? God supposedly made woman as an after-thought to man, to comfort him and to serve him, not as an equal, but as a helper. This, plus almost every reference to descendants which only mentions men, Adam and Noah, suggests that women are not equal, not even significant enough to be named. Multiple wives, husbands having children with maids and servants, the trading and giving of women and young girls as gifts and commodities, are all described as normal and proper behavior. Could this be a source that justifies sexism and abuse to women?

What about child abuse? Anyone threatening to stab and burn his son today, and coming within seconds of doing it because God told him to do so, would be institutionalized as insane. Yet Abraham is seen as being a faithful and a good father. The Bible is not alone in this respect. The Qur'an recognizes Abraham (Abrahim) as an especially important prophet for taking such a faithful position.

What about war and violence? In the big flood, god even destroys all humanity except for one chosen family because god says mankind has become wicked. God, in the story of Sodom and Gomorrah, destroys the entire city because he does not approve of their morals and they don't pray to him correctly. Were all the innocent children also wicked and sinful and deserved to die? If their god can declare war over such perceived behavior because the "infidels" don't believe in him as the correct God, men can surely follow this example and declare war against those who do not have the correct god.

I have only summarized a few stories from the first section of the Bible. It would be easy to go on for pages and pages describing all the brutality, cruelty, sexism, abuse, and violence that is approved of in this book. Many authors have done just that. It is popular these days to pick out statements from the Bible and point out how wrong such statements are, how they are examples of why not to believe in god. I have resisted doing this, as culturally inappropriate statements could probably be found in any two thousand year-old book. My goal is not to discredit belief in god. Believing the Bible to be a guide as how one should behave is the problem, and that is what I'm trying to discredit. Life was hard, basic resources were scarce, and slavery and violence were the norm. Thankfully, the world has moved on, and many of the world's people are now living in relative comfort, with basic resources, and with a different understanding of ethical behavior. The notion of nearly half the world using the Old Testament and the Torah as the essence of how they should lead their life is the scariest thing I can think of.

It is easy for me to dismiss these stories as the camp-fire tales that were handed down from generation to generation and finally written down in disparate pieces. They were written nearly two thousand years ago in a violent and male-dominated world, where slaves, selling of daughters, and fighting to keep ones possessions were common. In order to make the stories remembered, they were made to be extreme, and they were embellished, over and over, by each generation. The knowledge of the time was that of a flat world where disease was caused by demons. It is no wonder that it seemed possible to flood the world, to create all the diversity of life in one day, and all the other impossible things described in these books. But, I do not feel any need to believe them or to use any of them as a directive as to how I should live my life, or to even think of any of them as "the good book." But what about all those 2.1 billion Christians and the 14 million Jews whose daily actions and decisions on how to treat others in this "shrinking" world are based upon their "good book"?

I would ask you to pick up a copy of the Bible; you probably have one around someplace. Just take a few minutes, or even a few hours, and actually read it. If you are one of the many who think of themselves as Jewish or Christian but has not read this book, please do so. It may surprise you to learn what it actually says.

What about the role of violence for the 1.3 billion Muslims who base their faith on the Qur'an? Many scholars describe Islam as totalitarian, especially in its Islamic Law (Sharia) and in the Islamic notion of jihad, which has for its ultimate goal the conquest of the entire world in order to submit it to Allah as the one single authority. Sharia law strictly controls the entire life of the believer and the community. This is not a self-imposed control, freely given because of one's faith. The law-of-the-land is Islamic Law. It is all based upon the Qur'an, the Sunna of the Prophet, the Consensus (ijma) of the religious scholars, and the Method of Reasoning by Analogy (jiyas.) These four sources, which are all fixed, with the latest being the ijma (or the consensus), as the doctrine of infallibility in 900 CE. The faithful Muslims believe these four sources contain all knowledge that is or will ever be needed; it is a dead-end faith looking backward a thousand years into the past.

Islamic rules are valid by virtue of their mere existence and not because of any rational reason. Islamic law also requires the rules to be followed to the "letter" of the rule, not just to the "spirit" of the rule. The rules, which are many and are about everything in a believer's life, are absolute and fixed, based on the values of approximately the sixth century. Women are inferior, abuse is commonplace, and scientific progress is to be avoided.

When reading the Qur'an, I did not find nearly as many direct statements suggesting or requiring violence as I do in the Bible. I also do not find so prevalent the strong statements of inferiority of women and abuse of children that I had expected. I understand that prior to the Qur'an (early 600s CE), the customs in Arab areas for the treatment of women were even worse than now, with girls and women being used as work beasts and sexual objects. So, in that sense, Islam can be seen to have made progress in reducing the degree of gender abuse, as hard to believe as that may seem to us. Overall, it seems that much of what we see in fundamentalist Islam, as in all fundamentalist monotheism, are the extreme worst-case examples, but in predominantly Islamic countries, those extremes have become law and the norm for treatment of all people. As far as I can tell, it is like the worst of religious doctrine and dogma on steroids.

The Qur'an seems to include substantial portions that are based upon the Old Testament. For example, *"He said: 'O Adam! Inform them of their names . . .'* (2, 33), from the story of creation where Adam gives names to all the animals. But then it jumps around and talks about salvation and other stories from the Bible in no apparent order. The Qur'an is written to be directly doctrinal, not relating a history story from which readers can formulate their own meaning as is the case with some of the Bible.

Much of the Qur'an focuses on Abraham (Ibrahim), who is seen as an apostle. The Qur'an states the same idea as is found in the Christian Bible, that man is master over everything, and, therefore, the earth is to be used for man's pleasure. *"Allah is He Who created the heavens and the earth and sent down water from the clouds, then brought forth with it fruits as a sustenance for you, and He has made the ships subservient to you, that they night run their course in the sea by His command, and He has made the rivers subservient to you."* (14, 32) While the Qur'an was written many hundreds of years after the Bible, we find the same suggestions of violence against nonbelievers: *"Cursed: wherever they are found they shall be seized and murdered, a (horrible) murdering."* (33, 61) It is scary, to say the least, to believe that this kind of statement is god's literal commandment of action.

The Qur'an is also full of endless praise for Allah (god), which seems to be the main focus of the book. One wonders why it is necessary to repeat, over and over, how great, beneficent, and merciful he is. The constant statements of praise are rhythmic and sound hypnotic, which is what, I'm sure, was the intent. It is intended to be verbally learned, so that the message about how great Allah is will never be forgotten but always the first and last thought of every follower. In addition, the Qur'an jumps from first person (directly stated by god) in which much of it is written, to statements of "we," which I believe to be Muhammad and Allah, to a collective "they" format, all making it a little hard to keep straight. But reading it in English rather than Arabic likely misses much of what was intended.

Overall, the Qur'an presents the same message as the Christian and Jewish scriptures:

- Fear your god
- Hate everyone who is not like you
- Men are superior to women
- Violence and slavery are approved of, and finally

- Kill everyone who you cannot convert.

Because of the threat of extreme violence, as carried out in almost constant bomb attacks, in the 9/11 events, and in other suicide attacks, the concept of jihad deserves more attention. It is described in the Qur'an as "holy war," where attacks on the guilty are justified, and the attackers will be assured an immediate place in heaven. In reality, this is not that much different than Christian scripture. Again, the faithful Muslim can be easily convinced that this rationale for jihad is to be taken literally and that such action will lead to a glorious outcome.

The Qur'an says a war must either be carried out to defend yourself or to right a wrong. The problem for much of the world is that the orthodox Muslim sees the western world and specifically the United States as a "wrong" that they have the duty to right. Fundamentalist Islamic intolerance, based upon the current interpretation of the Qur'an and other Islamic holy books, make this religion the greatest threat to humankind that exists today.

As an ongoing example of such religious violence, in January of 2010, many incidents of arson and fire bombing occurred in Malaysia directed against Christian churches because of the use of the word "Allah" as a translation of the Christian word "God." Hindu temples were also destroyed, and a severed cow's head was paraded in the streets.

Violence against people because of religious differences is occurring every day and appears to be escalating. The Islamic abuse of women, the practice of limiting education opportunities to boys, the practice of mutilation of girls approaching puberty, and the practice of "honor killings" of children for moving outside the faith, are all directly related to the interpretation of scriptures. These are all a large part of the problem with religion today.

Violence is not the only problem that happens when people think their scriptures are the source of lessons for how to live. Let's look at institutionalized ignorance. All the way back to Plato and Socrates, people who try to advance knowledge have had to defend themselves against religion and scripture. Socrates, like so many wise men, was put to death because he threatened the religious leadership by independent thinking and questioning. Scripture tells us that knowledge is fixed, and everything we need to know is written in the holy books. Muslims, especially, follow this logic, with the Qur'an being the only book to be taught in many "schools." Islamic students spend hours memorizing the Qur'an in preparation for life. What can we expect from such an education, other than fifteen hundred year-old ignorance, about how the real world of today functions?

The conventional knowledge when these scriptures were written is extremely out of date, and the "wisdom" of the time included such things as:

- Demons were the cause of illness;
- People with schizophrenia were considered prophets;
- The earth was flat;
- The Sun revolved around the earth;
- Slavery was approved of and supported as natural;
- Women were inferior to men; and
- Answers to questions were found in the intestines of sacrificed animals.

Knowledge about how the world works has advanced in all domains except religion since the scriptures were written. Most people know these advances are valid and readily turn to science and its advancements for health care, entertainment, communication, and so much more. Nothing else, other than religion, is stuck in the belief that what was written almost two thousand years ago is perfect, true, and cannot be improved. When science proves that these scriptures are outdated and wrong, the faithful ignore the evidence and fight to stop the advance of knowledge. The outstanding discovery of evolution -- described by the National Academy of Sciences as "the most important concept in modern biology" --is still challenged by much of organized religion as merely a 'theory," meaning not any more real or valid than the theory of creationism. The evidence has been overwhelmingly consistent for over a hundred years that natural selection, based upon random variation, is what produces all the on-going variation on earth. Yet, all too often, educators have to fight their local school boards to teach children what every basic scientist knows to be essential to the foundation of our natural sciences today.

Ignorance could be more easily overlooked or corrected if, for example, evolution was disputed merely because the faithful did not know that there is overwhelming evidence that it is the best proven explanation of species creation. But they do know that. Virtually any literate person today has heard of or read about how Darwin's discovery and his book, The *Origin of Species,* explains fossils, dinosaur bones, and how life changes on this planet. Why do "the faithful" fight against such knowledge? Because it makes their creation story just that -- a story. If that story is wrong, how much else is wrong? It is naive to hate those who believe differently. It is ignorant to discriminate against homosexuals. It is ignorant to fight modern birth control methods which are proven to save lives and prevent the spread of AIDS. It is ignorant to stop medical research using Stem Cell techniques because, in some convoluted way, it goes against a two thousand year-old book. In these and so many other ways, scripture is used to prevent the advancement of knowledge and of compassionate care of humans on this planet.

Many followers of religious scripture are not even willing to take care of this earth. They will not listen to scientific information about what we are doing to our atmosphere and how it is impacting the earth. Preventing the pollution of our oceans and the deforesting of the jungles is not taken seriously because the scriptures say the earth is just here for man's use, and the earth is only temporary because the end is coming, and it will be glorious. Why take care of anything, or of anyone, if all you have to do is believe a story in an exceedingly old book promising that it will all work out in glorious revelation?

"Jesus saith unto him, I am the way, the truth, and the life: no man cometh unto the Father, but by me." (John 14:6) In other words, there is only one way, my way; everyone else is wrong. How much does this kind of thinking justify treating others as inferior, making the believer feel better and more elite than others? Is it the creation of someone who is merely a religious bigot, or is it more dangerous? In the Hindu faith, their 3000 year-old scriptures describe the ultimate prejudice toward others, the caste system, where your birth denotes your position in society. The Dalits (untouchables) fall into the lowest group, never allowed to associate with others and literally made outcasts for life. Is it no different than a Mormon father and mother disowning their teenage son or daughter for discovering that they are gay, or than a Jewish family restricting the social life of their daughter to a small Jewish group of contacts, or even a Muslim father killing his daughter because she dates an infidel. The faithful are all instructed to do so by their scriptures.

These actions all start with an attitude supported by scripture. When it is just an attitude, we call someone acting superior a bigot. When it involves the loss of something, and moves toward a legally outlawed action, we call it discrimination. I suspect it is discrimination in the United States when only someone identifying as a faithful member of an acceptable religion can run for a public office. Most atheists feel discriminated against because they lose many social opportunities; like the Dalits, they are shunned as bad and dangerous. But in reality, we atheists are actually lucky to be in the United States. While all major religion scriptures say it is the duty of the faithful to kill non-believers on contact, luckily for us this is illegal in America, at least for the time being.

In March of 2008, Dale and Leilani Neumann of Weston, Wisconsin, let their 11 year-old daughter die of untreated diabetes because they believed that scripture told them to reject modern medicine and to merely pray for a cure instead. She died a slow, painful, cruel, and completely unnecessary death. The Neumann's were found guilty of second-degree reckless homicide, but many agreed with their actions and are now working to get the decision overturned under the "faith-healing exemption" law of Wisconsin. Damage is done to defenseless children because of how scripture is interpreted every day, and the world looks away because it is religion.

I live with a woman, my wife, who has suffered mental child abuse because of the way she was forced to dress, wear her hair, dictated as to who she could date, and was never allowed to socialize like her school age friends. Being different because of her parent's religion has had a long and agonizing impact. She has become angry about her childhood experiences, where her parents' rules, based upon their fundamental interpretation of scripture, forced the entire family of eight children into an escape mode with lasting consequences for everyone. These are otherwise-loving parents who just put their religion ahead of using common sense.

No child has a religion. They are too young to understand the concepts of salvation; when they are "taught" their family's religion, it is scary and confusing to them. Here is what one girl said on the Internet about her childhood religious training: *"I spent many nights anxiety-ridden, sometimes crying myself to sleep. In my sleep, I would dream of the apocalypse, of being left behind in the rapture, of agonized friends screaming from hell, 'Why didn't you tell me?'"* And then there is the sensitive boy who, when a school friend tragically dies, believes that because his friend is not of his own faith, his friend will burn in hell for eternity. What price does that boy pay?

Actual physical child abuse related to religion is easy to locate as of late, with a steady stream of news about Catholic priests abusing boys and all the money being paid out by the Roman Catholic Church in case after case. The rumor is that this is just the tip of the iceberg, as other church leaders are yet to be identified with such actions. As tragic as this is, I believe it might be even worse to teach children the doctrines and scriptures of any of the monotheistic religions and convince them that these teachings are the literal Truth. What child can protect himself from such ideas? At minimum, they are confused about life. At worst they are terrorized by what is happening to everyone else and might happen to them because of an accidental death. Children's minds do not need to fear an invisible god, to be worried about whether or not they believe in the right god, or whether they are just being good enough to avoid burning in hell.

I cannot report personally on my emotions about what scripture said to me as a child. I was fortunate to be raised with no fears of invisible gods or of serving a supernatural deity that has power over my life. I was taught to ask questions, to be kind, to be respectful of my elders, to think about things the best I could and then go play with my friends. I have to admit that I thought it was silly that one of my friends could not eat meat on Fridays, and my mother always had to remember this when he stayed overnight at our home. As my friend and I got older, and we would drink too many beers, I would occasionally trick him into ordering a pizza with pepperoni on it and then remind him it was Friday. I got an extra piece that way.

I have already said plenty about scripture and homosexuality. It is bigotry, discrimination, child abuse, ignorance and ultimately violence. Why this group gets singled out for so much hatred is difficult to understand. To say I get upset about this is a tremendous understatement. All this anger toward gays needs to be challenged publicly and loudly.

What can we say about anger? We know it comes from fear. Why many of those who believe in scripture are so afraid of homosexuality is a matter for psychologists or other specialists. It is easy to find scripture that supports their angry attitude, but why is it there? Are they some specific threat to monotheistic gods? Whatever the reason, it is time to give it up. It seems that homosexuals have been part of the primate world forever and surely will be for the foreseeable future, so what is the problem?

Gender abuse based on scripture is supported and regularly reinforced. In the West, it is easy for us to see it within Islam. One of the most revered Muslim theologians, Imam Ghazali, said,

"Marriage is a form of slavery. The woman is man's slave, and her duty, therefore, is absolute obedience to the husband in all that he asks of her person. A woman, who at the moment of death enjoys the full approval of her husband, will find her place in paradise." The Qur'an and the reported Hadith are full of statements such as, *"Women are more harmful to men than anything else. The husband may forbid his wife to leave the home. Women are domestic animals; beat them. Women are half devils."*

Under Islamic or Sharia law:
>   - A woman cannot divorce a man, but a man can divorce by only saying the words, "I divorce you" three times – and it is legally binding.
>   - custody of children after years 7-9 goes automatically to the father.
>   - wife beating is legal, of all four legal wives.
>   - there is no community property and no
>   support for the wife if:
>   - the woman is "rebellious;"
>   - she leaves the home without permission from husband;
>   - she refuses to have sex with him;
>   - she is too young to have sex, marriage is legal at age 9.
>   - she is too sick to have sex; or
>   - she has been raped by another man.

What about Christian scripture? Are women seen as equal to men? *"Wives, be subject to your husbands, as to the Lord. For the husband is the head of the wife as Christ is the head of the church ..."* (Ephesians 5:22-23). We should expect no more equality in scripture than what were the normal customs of the time. This is not the model we want to use for how we should live our lives today.

As an educator, I have a strong reaction to those who do not provide the best information available to our youth and who let scripture interfere in the process of teaching factual knowledge. Abstinence-only instruction is an example of direct government involvement supporting religious bias in public policy. This "education" is often required in order for school districts to obtain funds from federal sources. In 2009, fifty million dollars were given in federal funding for abstinence-only programs in the United States. Does it work? Several studies, as well as common sense, tell us that it does not work; in fact, it leads to increased teen pregnancy. Texas, which has an extremely high rate of teen pregnancy, receives more federal funding for abstinence education than any other state. A Texas Network study found that more than 94 percent of Texas school districts "do not give students any human sexuality instruction beyond abstinence." In addition, 40 percent of Texas secondary schools' sexuality curriculum contains factual errors regarding condoms and sexually transmitted diseases. Many school districts go so far as to teach that students need to ask themselves if God approves of whom they date; some even teach students that they should always make Jesus their first love. This is not education; it is propaganda and indoctrination. As stated above, there is no place for religion to have influence in public education institutions. It is against the law; it is bad for our country; it is bad for students.

Who is it that has been attacking health workers at abortion clinics across this country? It is radical fundamental Christians who get the idea from scripture that they need to act in violent ways to stop what is, in fact, a legal procedure. No thoughtful person wants to see unwanted pregnancies, but it is the decision of our courts that a prospective mother has the right to control her own body. In Roe v. Wade, the court noted that, *"We need not resolve the difficult question of when life begins. When those trained in the respective disciplines of medicine, philosophy, and theology are unable to arrive at any consensus, the judiciary, at this point in the development of man's knowledge, is not in a position to speculate as to the answer."* With respect to the State's important and legitimate interest in potential life, the "compelling" point is that point at which there is possible viability of life for the fetus. This is because the fetus then is presumed to have the capability of meaningful life outside the mother's womb. We need more education about safe, rational ways of preventing unwanted pregnancies; we don't need ideas from two thousand years ago to incite people to violence.

Summary of the Problem

It is remarkably easy for human beings to believe in the supernatural. Our species has probably been doing it for fifty thousand years, or as long as we have had language. To believe in demons, ghosts, and gods seems to be natural. As people moved from tribal hunter-gathers to stationary villages, these spirits also changed to a pantheon of polytheistic gods. When larger societies developed, forming countries and numerous city states with a common identity, it became popular and politically expedient for their religion to evolve to be framed around a monotheistic god. Three of these monotheistic gods were invented in the desert of the Middle East, between 1,000 and 3,000 years ago, and they have become the selected deities for about half the people on earth today. Each of these three monotheistic faiths has its own god (Jehovah, Jesus, Allah) and its own holy book. All of these books are, for the most part, based upon the original stories about Abraham and his God.

From our modern perspective, these holy books were written in a culture of violence, sexual abuse, child abuse, and slavery, and with a decidedly limited understanding about what are now the natural sciences. Ignorance about the world and how it works has resulted in many stories using the idea of god(s) to explain the unexplainable and to solve the mysteries of life and death. Scripture in these holy books provided stability through the consistency of the dogmas and ritualistic practices of each faith. Prophets provided examples about how to live a "god-fearing" life within the culture, and they even created some of the written content, in the case of Muhammad. Furthermore, these books teach how to be a faithful member of the particular religion; they contain rules, commandments, and laws of conduct that were based upon the culture of the time.

The reason I focus on the scriptures of these religions rather than on their gods is that the books are palpable objects that are reproducible. They form and reinforce the foundations, the content, of religions; the gods only exist within the minds of the followers. As far as I can tell, the gods have never caused any harm to anyone. (Even though some believers say that god creates floods, plagues, etc. as retribution, it has never been documented.) Yet believers, following the directions of their scriptures, have killed millions, destroyed cities, invaded countries, and impeded the advancement of knowledge for thousands of years. It is immutable scripture that keeps a religion and its adherents prisoners of the past. The belief that it cannot be changed and that it is "true" for all times is what keeps religion from evolving with new knowledge. This immutability is what keeps the followers of all major faiths from solving new problems with new information, and it's what keeps them from moving forward toward a unified world community of peace.

To the mind of a believer, the concept of a god can provide comfort when that person is in a community of believers. A god often is used as the answer to the big "why" questions of life. Believers seem to be at peace in such discussions or in prayer with their god. In essence, a god and the relationship a believer has with that god, is not the problem. When people talk to their god, they speak from the point of view of their culture and their morals, and they usually are asking for help in figuring out life's problems. From my non-believing point of view, this is not really different from when I am having a conversation with my wonderful wife (where I do all the talking and she just listens) until I finally figure out what I'm going to do. As a vocal extrovert, I often need to hear myself talk. I wonder if prayer might be similar.

Not all conversations with a god are so positive. People who hear their god tell them to do violent and terrible things we call insane; often they have schizophrenia and are seriously mentally ill. Thinking that scripture is the literal word of a god, and that it is true and must be followed is also not healthy or rational.

The scriptures of these major monotheistic religions are the problem when they are thought to be inerrant, unchangeable, and that they contain the lessons of how one should act and think. I combine all the scriptures in the Torah, the Bible, the Qur'an, and the Book of Mormon in this statement because, from my point of view, they are quite similar.

Each of these books has shared, problematic features:

1.) They are Intolerant of any other faith or anyone different than themselves. They teach prejudice and bigotry by condemning others for being different in any way other than what they believe to be their right way. This single-minded disdain of all others eventually becomes hatred and violence. The hatred results in suicide bombings, wars, genocide, and, in our nuclear age, could even end all human life on earth. This religious intolerance phenomenon is what many believe to be the greatest threat to humanity that exists today.

2.) They all place man as the beneficiary of this earth, to use it predominantly for his satisfaction, with no responsibility for the well-being of the planet itself or any other, non-human living thing on it. As I traveled through some Moslem countries, I could only conclude that there is no concern about the long-range environmental impact of their living styles. For example, in one Muslim country, I personally observed garbage and dead animals literally floating through the waterways of the biggest cities and passing right by what has been the tallest building in the world. They also purposely set forest fires to clear the jungle, which caused thousands of people to be ill and many to die from the smoke and ash. These religious cultures operate on the belief that because Allah said he made this earth for man, and that man is its master, he is free to take, take, and take; every other living thing "below man" is put there for his use.

The Bible provides a similar message, *"Take no thought for tomorrow. Tomorrow will take thought of the things of itself."* After all, the end is coming soon. For the last seven hundred or so generations, we have been waiting for the end of times; maybe we just missed it, or we're wrong about that. Maybe we should start taking care of this planet for the next 700 generations!

3.) All these scriptures foster gender discrimination, where women are inferior to men. A woman is described as an after-thought of god to provide comfort to a man. She was guilty of the first sin, and thus, the reason for all our sin; she was hardly worthy of being named in the historical accounts of human development. "Man is the king of his castle;" and, "A woman's place is to be continually barefoot and pregnant." Where did such ideas come from? Yes, from the scriptures.

4.) Child abuse is often the outcome of religious groups' interpretation of scripture. It is easy for us to see how this is so within the Islamic faith, but I think it is sanctioned in all the major religious books written during a time where treatment of children was decidedly different from what we accept today. Selling of daughters was acceptable; they were more like livestock, to be used as property for the parents' benefit. Furthermore, the mere practice of indoctrinating children into believing scripture as literal truth, when they are not old enough to analyze it for themselves, is abusive. Children in poor, Muslim countries are particularly vulnerable to the old teachings in Islamic "Madrassa schools," where they are indoctrinated into a life of hatred and distrust.

5.) All of the monotheistic scriptures discourage rational and scientific inquiry and the advancement of knowledge. When science threatens the "truth" of the scriptures, the "solution" is to delegitimize science and prevent the advancement of research; at various times throughout history, the solution has lead to the killing of those who question and reason. Religions and their scriptures are responsible for the dark ages, which literally stopped the advancement of medicine, physical science, astronomy and many other sciences for hundreds of years. We see the same argument going on today; if scripture suggests a topic is off limits, we must give up trying to get funding for research. How long did it take to see AIDS as anything other than a homosexual disease where god was giving to "them" what they deserved? Pat Roberts was reported to say that the terrible earthquake in Haiti in January of 2010 happened because the Haitian people had offended his God in some way; such ignorance of tectonic plate movement and the physical forces of this planet are just another example of how fundamental ignorance is spread to religions' followers.

It well could be that the world, as we know it, will end because of hatred and violence between religions, because the scriptures of each of the three big, monotheistic religions teach hatred towards everyone who believes differently. Major wars are already being fought -- the Fight Against Evil, the War on Terror, the Fight Against Terrorism. Why doesn't anyone point out and respond to what is really going on? We hate "the other" because they believe differently than we do! The "we" keeps changing, the belief keeps changing, but, in fact, it all can be reduced to the simple, pervasive premise -- "accept my holy book as true or I will kill you."

If we don't destroy humanity by nuclear terrorism, then we can look forward to serious and persistent conflicts because of overcrowding; populations will continue to grow beyond the capacity of the planet to support them, in part because scripture says god wants us to go forth and multiply. Or, perhaps we will suffer serious environmental problems of radiation damage from the sun, or of flooding from overheating the planet, or we will eventually be destroyed due to disturbing the climate balance, all because scripture said this earth was here for man to exploit and abuse.

Another possible outcome, if nuclear destruction does not occur first, is that the growth of Islam will take over the West, and we will all be under Sharia law. Freedom will be gone, we will stop the advancement of science, we will return to slavery, we will treat women as animals, and we'll all bow to the east or be killed. Europe is now feeling this terribly real threat. The violence is escalating there from and toward the Muslim communities. My Christian friends, even in America, can see this threat and are quick to say "let's fight". After all, those Muslims believe in the wrong book. What they do not seem to realize is that all the books are just that, books, among many that are to be read, thought about, and balanced in our ever-advancing knowledge about what makes this world a better place for all living things.

The picture ahead, if we continue to look two thousand years into the past for our guide on how to treat each other and how to take care of our planet, is not particularly bright. Scripture has not served us well for a long time; it is time for a change. The crucial question is, can we change, or are we stuck with the power of "blind faith," based upon stories of a bunch of tribes fighting in the desert thousands of years ago?

Part Four - - Some Possible Solutions

Can Religions Evolve?

Can religions evolve to become more modern and to show tolerance for those who believe differently?

In essence, this is the crucial question -- Is it possible to solve the "big problem" I mentioned above, to overcome the real possibility that humanity might be destroyed by religious hate? Is it hopeless?

No, it is not yet hopeless; religions do evolve and change. But, if you ask the more fundamentalist followers of almost all the major religions, you will be told that their religion is clearly immutable; it does not change, and it is true now, and it always will be the same. Many traditionalists or fundamentalists of each religion seem to believe that there is value in staying pure and in getting back to the basics of scripture. In some strange way, it is common to think that old is good and change is bad. One of the most common beliefs of all religions is that it is fixed in time. Even when change does occur, it is explained as "further revelation" or "completion" of the faith. This is an important issue in considering solutions to the problems of religion today. If religions can not change peacefully along with societal changes, we are either doomed to live in the past, or we have to go through a major societal upheaval each time people demand change in their faith to fit evolving cultures.

It is clear that the god of Abraham, Jehovah, or Yahweh, is not the same god that is worshipped by modern Jews. The god of the New Testament is also very different. Jesus, the new god, is considerably more forgiving than Jehovah. Then, we have to consider the whole devil or Satan business, which was such a prominent part of the ancient monotheistic faiths, where maintaining a balance between "good" and "evil" was popular. Much of this need for a frightened vigilance about Evil has been forgotten by today's faithful except in the most fundamentalist groups, where it still thrives. Another change is that most faithful people now think they can have a personal relationship with their god. He (it is still a "he" most of the time) will listen directly to his followers and have a personal relationship with each believer, unlike in the dark ages where there needed to be an intermediary, a priest who was the only one able to have the ear of the lord. This shift is primarily a result of the growth of literacy, fostered by the invention of the printing press.

We can all see many ways that faiths change over time to suit the needs of the believers. There have been many instances where the Pope simply changes the rules if they do not fit any more, or if the old ways will not work to control the masses. For example, in 1999, the Pope defined Hell as a mental state, not an actual place; but for all those who went to Hell prior to that, they must still be burning in a real hell? Most religious leaders admit now that the earth is more than 6,000 years old and that Latin is not really the language of god, as they earlier insisted upon in order to intimidate and impress the masses. So it seems that religion can adapt in some cases, at least, to meet the needs of new customers when it is faced with a risk of losing followers.

Another way religion evolves is through the development of "spin-offs" or the fragmenting into different variations. Mormonism is an example, which has become one of the major religions of the world, yet is clearly based upon the Bible. All the protestant varieties of Christianity are similar "schism" varieties. Luther decided it was okay to have a personal relationship with god and got mad at the Pope. Calvin wanted the church to run the government, and he also believed that the sacrament was being administered incorrectly by Luther. The Baptists did not agree about when a child should be or could be "saved" and how the saving should be done. The Seventh Day Adventists wanted to use Saturday as the correct day of rest, as well as a number of other minor changes.

More recently, we see a change toward informality in some Christian groups, where popular music, everyday clothing, and having entertainment in "worship" services; this informality is becoming the variable that sets them apart from the more formal, traditional denominations. We also now see the "megachurch" with more than 2,000 worshipers attending weekly in one building. In the United States, these megachurches have grown to more than 47,000 weekly worshipers at one site, for example, and they have numerous specialized ministry positions to handle each family member's needs. Entertainment is also offered, media extravaganzas occur weekly, and they literally try to meet all the social needs of their urban memberships. They are becoming the church, the country club, the theater, and the family therapist, all rolled into a one-stop shop, and tax deductible to boot.

The Shiites of the Islamic faith have branched off from the earlier, main-stream Islamic faith, based on disagreement about the proper leadership determined by the linage from Mohamed. There are at least four different "schools of Islam," all teaching the faithful a slightly different version of the Qur'an. Some Islamic countries like Malaysia have found ways to live in reasonable harmony with their Hindu and Christian citizens, even if it took a long and bloody war to reach that point. This blending was facilitated by their close cultural contact with the more tolerant eastern religions. Judaism has also evolved with major divisions, such as the Orthodox, Reform, and Conservative or Reconstructionist versions.

Fostering revolution and military overthrow is still a big issue in religion. Much of the middle east is in a major struggle over what seems to be political, not religious, control of people and resources; but, just under the surface is the continuing intolerance by religious leaders, so evident and yet not talked about. It has become painfully obvious that the United States does not understand the religious culture of this part of the world. When faith is the foundation of hatred and political instability, pouring money or bombs onto the problem is not the answer. This approach usually does not result in an effective or long-lasting solution. No doubt these are complex issues, where hatred toward others, ultimately based on scripture, exists; when these people are divided by political boarders, the result is all too often war, death, and substantial destruction.

It is clear that over the last several thousand years of history, religion has changed. It slowly, and with considerable conflict, tends to reflect the changes that occur in society. The influence of religion has become more centralized as societies moved from hunter/gatherers into city states and larger political units. As literacy grew, subgroups gained strength and independence, resulting in divergent protestant groups. We have seen the ideological splintering of cults and radical fundamentalist groups, and now we see a trend in evolving megachurches, attempting to meet a wide array of social and entertainment needs of their members. As much as the followers of all the major religions want to assert that their religious doctrines are immutable and will never change, they all change, one way or another.

What about changing religion by just starting a new religion? I stated earlier that there are two new religions started every day. What happens to them? Most do not thrive; they attract so few followers that they are not even considered a cult, and they just fade away. Yet some do continue and grow as new options. In the United States, we have Scientology as an example of a new religion with many followers. Scientology was started by L. Ron Hubbard using his book, Dianetics: The Modern Science of Mental Health. It is about "spiritual healing," but it also contains a theme of perfection-seeking where a believer moves on, much like the Buddhists, to a nirvana. As a modern faith, it has elements of a "kind of science" and a moral code, along with some faith-based science fiction space elements.

Another modern idea is to transmute belief in UFO activity into a kind of religion. The Heaven's Gate group believed that humans were plant-like vessels for aliens to use and to be eventually taken to a higher form after a sacred suicide. This was, loosely, a combination of some parts of Christianity (Revelation) and space alien beliefs. Another new religion, this time in Japan, is the Aum Shinrikyo sect. They came to the world's attention when they released the nerve gas sarin into the subways in Tokyo a few years ago. They were heavy on suffering, not only of their members, but also of others. It seems that we tend to hear only about these extreme examples of new faiths; but more reasonable, supporting, and loving new faiths are also likely out there and could be effective in encouraging and realizing religious change.

Major Change to Solve the Big Problems

Many believe that stability and peace can only occur when significant change occurs within the major religions themselves. If this is true, the vital question is, can the modern monotheistic believers decide to change their practice of these faiths and stop hating, and ultimately killing, each other?

John Shelby Spong, a retired Episcopal bishop, wants to do just that. He feels that it is time to modernize the Christian religion, to stop thinking about the Bible as "the word of god," because it was not written by god. It is obviously full of contradictions, and it is terribly violent, sexist, homophobic, and full of outright stupid statements. (Well, I might have added that last one). He says it is not reasonable to take literally the writings that made up all the books of the Bible. They were orally shared stories among largely illiterate tribes of people, first put to paper a long time after the events reported, and these stories were then rewritten, modified, and translated by humans. In addition, they just don't fit our modern world; in many cases they were terrible, destructive statements toward their own women and children and as well as the neighboring tribes, even when they were written. He also identifies the Christian religion as the motivating force for how we have almost ruined our environment, over-populated our planet, and created much of the hate in the world today. He says that he is a serious Christian believer and scholarly religious thinker who wants to save the Christian faith with a major update.

What Bishop Spong wants to help us all to do is look inward to find a new, loving inter-religion-based god, to extract out the good parts of the Bible and focus on them, and ignore all the hate and bigotry that people have found in many of the scriptures. This is a huge change that the good bishop is hoping will somehow manifest. It has become obvious to him that this must happen, both to save the planet and to save his religion. Personally, I think it would be difficult to keep just the good parts of the Bible and reframe the idea of a jealous, war-oriented sky god into a universal, personal, internal god voice who works within each person to help them live with love for themselves and all others.

Overall, I do agree with Bishop Spong that if we do not do something soon about the literal, scripture-based beliefs that exist in these major, monotheistic religions, we will overpopulate to the point of constant conflict, and we will kill each other or at least make the environment unlivable for humans. He attributes all of these terrible outcomes to the literal following of the Christian scriptures.

Perhaps Bishop Spong is right to try and keep a common-named but newly defined God in the picture; people seem to need one, and Christianity

already diverse enough so that a positive-
ated version might just be possible. Again,
ving in and of itself is not the problem. It is
ing the literal words of a jealous and vengeful
created by man over 2000 years ago in a
sperate time that is the problem.

What Spong is suggesting sounds to me a lot like
the Baha'i faith, where they are trying to unite all
faiths and focus on peace and justice. The Baha'i
spiritual community is already world-wide and has
over seven million members. The Baha'i teaches
that all faiths contain the same basic spiritual
truths, just expressed in different ways. They have
eliminated sexual, racial and class prejudice in
their doctrines and have established a functioning,
democratic way of operating their faith. And best of
all, they don't want to kill anyone if someone
outside their group does not believe the way they
do. From this example, significant religious change
does seem possible.

I highly recommend Greg Mortenson's book, *Three
Cups of Tea*. He is the one person who has done
more to solve the critical problem of hate and
mistrust between people with different beliefs than
anyone I know. He has personally shown how an
individual can make a difference. Mortenson has
built schools all across the remote areas of
Pakistan, and also now Afghanistan, to educate
children and create a better life in remote villages.
While he has supported providing a basic
education for all, he is especially focused on giving
girls a chance at an education; he says that

educating women holds the key to future stability and reason in Muslim areas. My favorite quote from his book is, *"The enemy is ignorance. The only way to defeat it is to build relationships with these people, to draw them into the modern world with education and business. Otherwise, the fight will go on forever."* Mortenson is unique in that he is able and willing to endure the hardships of living among the members of remote, mountain villages in Pakistan while demonstrating respect for the villagers and their ways. He genuinely understands that love, intelligence, and human decency exist among all populations and cultures, regardless of religion or race.

I have often said that, if our foreign aid programs could educate girls to read, it would demonstrate that girls can be successful and could create incentive for change. It would cause the movement needed to end discrimination and abuse against females. As Mortenson has found, once girls have a chance for education, they will lead the way to better health for their community and a better standard of living for their families. Literacy, education, and a chance to live happily, with the hope for a better life for their children, could dramatically reduce hatred, discrimination, and all the unnecessary suffering that exists.

Our goal must be for the people of the world to coexist as a global community with kindness, compassion, and cultural respect for each other. Our world is getting smaller, in the sense that we can now more readily communicate with each other, trade our goods, and share the best parts of each of our cultures. We can learn from each other; we can appreciate what each culture has to offer. Just imagine not having Chinese food, or German beer, Irish music, or French wine and so many other delightful things from so many wonderful places. We could all celebrate our diversity in peace, except for one significant fact -- that over half of the people of the world want to kill their neighbors because they believe in a different god.

The bottom line is that we need to update the major monotheistic religions of today. We need to change the selection and interpretation of scriptures so that tolerance and equality is taught as the loving and ethical behavior of all faiths. We need to see women and men as equals. We need to see this planet as our home and something we are responsible to protect. We need to see homosexuality as just part of the differences that occur naturally among humans. We need to protect, nurture, and educate children so they can think like independent, rational individuals. Most of all, we need to stop hating and killing other people just because they believe in supernatural things differently than we do. In a rational world, this change would normally occur because we are continually learning from each other to be common, communicating people of one planet. But instead, because of the scriptures, frozen two thousand years in the past, our spiritual believers are mired down reading stories supporting slavery, selling daughters, killing infidels, and hating everyone who is different.

Under these monotheistic faiths, societies develop hatred and go to war over how to perpetuate the power of their faiths, even when they believe in the same god, such as the conflicts between the Protestants and the Catholics in Ireland, and between the Sunnis and the Shiites in Iraqi. The hatred that is fostered poisons their minds and closes the door to rational reason.

To summarize, here are some options that could help solve this problem:

1.) The current religions could evolve because their members push for modernization and demand change. The best of the current religions are kept; the old and unworkable are dropped. People would, in essence, see that change is needed and that the ancient scriptures are not working. They would "get it" that, to achieve a world-wide balance of respect and tolerance, the old scriptures need updating.

2.) A new schism or offshoot religion replaces each of the old ones, based upon a loving and compassionate god which is not intolerant of others. Again, more believers are needed to move into this new offshoot religion. They need to be uncomfortable with how their current faith is working and want something better that makes more sense to them.

3.) An entirely new religion is started, and it takes over as more people move to it. There does not seem to be any shortage of dynamic and charismatic leaders available to create new religions.

Five steps we can take as individuals to change from entrenched intolerance to an enlightened humanity:

First, we need to start talking about this problem. We need to acknowledge that much of the hatred people feel toward each other comes from their religious scriptures. Distrust, fear, anger and hate are all foundational parts of the scriptures of the major monotheistic religions. While there may be a lot of good things in those scriptures, the intolerance, bigotry, sexism, and child abuse continues to be perpetuated by the faithful. It is necessary to talk about these unacceptable behaviors and relate them to their source when they are clearly fostered by religion.

As a first step, we could start asking those who base their faith on these religions to look carefully at what their scriptures actually say. I have read literally dozens of books that constantly list all the statements of hatred found in the Bible and the Qur'an. They are overwhelmingly influential, and we need to acknowledge this. These were statements made during a hard and desperate time in history. Let's help the faithful see them for what they are -- oral allegories and exaggerations written down hundreds of years after they were reported to have happened. They were translated numerous times and then edited into one overall compilation, mostly for political control purposes. It is okay to talk about religion, to have an opinion about this subject. It should no longer be taboo to do so; it is essential that we bring this immense problem out of the politically correct shadows and into the light of open discussion.

Why is it that we cannot talk about religion? It is all around us; it impacts our policies, our finances and our social structures. Why should the faithful be afraid to talk about how their ideas are influenced by scripture? If they are not afraid, why not discuss it? If they are afraid, their fear needs to be addressed. We should all show respect for other ways of seeing things; maybe we discredists can learn something. We all learn by open discussion and can benefit from it. Religion must not be out of bounds in this regard. We all can learn from open honest dialogue. I might find other ways of looking at scripture; I could change my point of view, I'm open to the opportunity to learn. Only those who "believe" that scripture is perfect and unchangeable will shun open discussion and maintain the old ways of imposing their fixed beliefs on others.

Furthermore, if we point out that a prayer is not appropriate at a nonreligious event, we are not being disrespectful. We are being honest and straightforward that it does not belong there, at least in America. At any nonreligious event, where differences of faith, or no faith, are present, everyone needs to be respected. Faith is not universal, there is not one correct form, and no one has the right to subject others unwillingly to their beliefs. It is time to talk about it openly and to stand up to it when it is forced upon people, saying "STOP! That is not right."

It is time we encourage our media to report clearly when religious hatred is at the heart of terrorism, abuse, or war. Sure, politics are important and play a role in most news stories, but we rarely hear a report that clearly says that the cause of the behavior was that the terrorist bomber wanted to kill as many infidels as possible and that their religious clergy were clearly a significant influence over the individuals who performed the terrorist activity.

A few days ago I listened to a lengthy televised CBS special report titled Women in Afghanistan. It included coverage of how these women are abused, how women can be imprisoned just by the word of their husbands, how young girls are still not being educated, and how men think it is acceptable to keep their wives and daughters prisoners in their homes. Not once during the entire report was religion mentioned, and they never said WHY this was happening to women in this country. The pendulum has swung way too far toward being "sensitive" to religions. It is time to talk openly and candidly about where these ideas come from and why they are being continued.

Many of my friends and family cannot talk about their faith in any explanatory way. I don't know if they truly know what their holy books say. I don't know if they believe that the statements of hate in these books are actually the "word of god." My fear is that they might believe that these 1600 to 2000 year old messages of hate are somehow true and should still be followed. Even if they don't think they are to be followed literally, do they nevertheless think these messages should guide how they live and treat others? Even though I do not personally believe in a god, I can allow them to do so, and I do that gladly. I know it gives them comfort; and why would I want to take that away? What I do want to take away is the intolerance that the faithful have for the rest of humanity that does not subscribe fully to the same faith. I want the suspicion, discrimination, and prejudice against those who believe in a different god, or in no god, to go away. What I want is to take a step toward genuine "peace on earth" which is something more than a holiday phrase! I will start asking my religious family and friends what their scriptures say about equality of women, tolerance of other faiths, and respect for those who do not believe.

I will continue to ask about and talk about religion, and I will be respectful toward those who believe in a supernatural god. As I have said, believing in a god is not the problem; it is following the messages of hate that their religious scriptures encourage that is the problem. I will also be clear that the messages of hate, bigotry, slavery, and abuse found in these holy books have no place in a global village where we all need to coexist in peace.

How can we do this? Nobody wants to be ridiculed for their beliefs, nor should they be. Nonbelievers are no smarter or better than believers. Just because someone has not learned about evolution, anthropology, or geology does not make them bad. It is likely they were taught to avoid these topics, to reject them without consideration, and instead to make decisions based upon a 1600 year old book. I'm not encouraging anybody to be rude, disrespectful, or to act in an unkind manner. I am demanding to be free from their judgment and intentions to impose their beliefs on me. I'm suggesting we all get involved in the conversation about the "problems with religion today."

Many years ago as a student, I had the opportunity to tutor a bright (and attractive) college girl in an undergraduate humanities class. Her father was a minister, and she was failing her biology and evolution courses. As hard as I tried to help her, she just could not allow herself to accept or even remember the information for the tests. Now, I understand that it was a conflict between what she had been taught all her life about creation and what modern science currently knows to be the truth. Because it was easy for me to learn this subject, and I was fascinated by anthropology (Desmond Morris -- the author of the Naked Ape -- became my favorite author,) it did not make me better or smarter than she. That year, I almost flunked my "bone head" algebra for the second time. My point is that, because someone has not had an opportunity to learn or consider another way of looking at "the big questions," that is no reason to be rude or feel superior. After all, nonbelievers are by far the minority. But then, all believers of any faith are also a minority, as none of the religions is a majority. It is my hope that all nonbelievers would get off their high horses, listen to believers, understand why they believe what they do, ask questions about why they follow their holy books, and finally, politely offer some information that might help counteract the hatred and intolerance that is so common in religious doctrines. As Thomas Jefferson said, *"Question with boldness even the existence of god."*

Second, we can stop feeling guilty about not being a believer. Everybody was born an atheist or a discredist. Religion is taught; people learn to be religious. I suspect it is true that, as an evolved human, we are susceptible to believing in a supernatural god. It just seems natural to accept the supernatural gods and spirits, as it has seemed for thousands of generations before. But a discredist or a nonbeliever is not a bad person; he or she is not unprincipled or immoral because they do not believe in supernatural deities. Well over a billion people do not believe in a god, and they are not inferior to the billions who believe in thousands of different gods.

Prejudices against nonbelievers should be challenged and not tolerated. Nonreligious events and organizations should not be including prayer or any other religious element in their activities. In the United States, everyone has the right to attend any church, mosque, temple or synagogue they choose, but it is insulting to nonreligious people to be expected to participate in religious activities where religion is inappropriate. In short, it is time to "come out of the closet" and be recognized as a discredist.

No nonbeliever ever committed a murder or killed their children because they did not believe. Being a skeptic, when there is no evidence for thinking something is true, is just thinking for your self. I do not feel embarrassed any longer to say, "No, I do not believe in a god." It does not make me a bad or unprincipled person.

In all countries, a large portion of educated people do not believe in the supernatural. I could find lists that would go on for pages of famous people who do not believe in a god or gods; but what is important is that there are millions of ordinary people, like you and me, who are willing to say, "No, I don't believe in a god." These are good people who donate money and give their time to helping others. Very likely, they even help religious people without caring that they are or are not religious. Spurred by the horrific suffering in Haiti after the January 2010 earthquake, the Richard Dawkins Foundation for Reason and Science (RDFRS) has joined forces with 20 other free-thought groups to collect donations for nonreligious relief organizations. This is just one example of caring nonbelievers who have given untold millions of dollars to help others in times of crisis.

Another thing we can all do to help change how we take religion for granted is to become aware of our "Christian" language. So much of our language is about religion and specifically about Christianity. It is almost impossible to listen to music without hearing a reference to god or the "good book." We all say things that are suggesting of religion.

Today, I caught myself saying, in reference to something that is likely to occur, "that is as sure as hell." I literally started laughing at how silly that sounds, coming from me. I do not mean to merely stop using what is considered religious profanity, which we should all stop doing anyway, but to pay attention to how often our everyday language refers to religion. We take it for granted as normal conversation, not noticing how it reinforces the idea that being religious is good and not being religious is bad. Just pay attention to what you hear and say; I would guess you will be surprised how often religion-based language is used in our everyday conversation and how often you use it yourself. As a starting point, just notice how often you hear the phrase "god-fearing" as a positive statement about somebody. Then ask yourself, "Why is that a positive thing?"

Don't forget that to stop feeling guilty about not believing is not a license to feel superior to those who do believe. The goal is justice and tolerance, not superiority or intolerance.

I love my family members who are religious. I also love my friends who are religious, and in no way do I feel superior because I do not share their beliefs. As I have said many times, believing is not the problem; it is the hatred and intolerance that comes from outdated scriptures that need to change. People who believe in a religion are, for the most part, good citizens, kind and intelligent people who have made a decision to accept some things on faith, without objective analysis, and it makes them feel good. If, as a nonbeliever, I can ask them to accept me as a good person, then I can accept them as a good and equal person who just happens to get something from their belief that I don't understand or comprehend.

Third, we can learn and teach that believing in a god does not have to mean that the believer needs to kill everyone he cannot convert. Many religions of the world have tolerance toward people who see god or gods differently. Anyone who wants to continue believing in a personal deity does not need to give it up in order to reject the toxic parts of major monotheistic scriptures. If a god can exist for hundreds of different religions, then perhaps there is a loving, peaceful way to find that god in a new and modern religious organization. The Baha'i faith, as I have mentioned, is an example, where they have tried to respect all the previous messiahs, to build on equality for everyone (including women,) and to foster peace across all faiths. Currently they fall short of full acceptance of homosexuality and for women in their highest ranks, but they do show that a monotheistic faith can make enormous strides toward equality. Here is what they say about equality: *"The Bahá'í teachings promote the elimination of all forms of prejudice and uphold equal dignity and respect for all peoples, regardless of their racial, ethnic, religious or national background. Equality of men and women, the elimination of extremes of poverty, and wealth and economic justice for all peoples, universal education, and the dignity of the individual are central Bahá'í principles."* I'm not at all inclined to promote a particular religion. But it is refreshing to hear about a contemporary religion which is trying to solve some of the obvious problems of many faiths today. Members of the Baha'i faith elect their local leaders in a popular election, and women are encouraged to run for offices equally with men. They work to solve specific problems that they identify in their own community, and their members are encouraged to operate local units of the faith differently, depending on their local culture. I am impressed.

It will take great effort to convince the people of the traditional monotheistic faiths that they have other options and that such a tolerant faith could provide the same social benefits and still allow maintaining a belief in a supernatural god that is modern, with respect for all people. To me, believing in a god does not seem to implicitly cause any problem, and it is very refreshing to hear about at least one growing faith that is trying to be equitable and caring for all people. I know many people who are dissatisfied with their particular denomination or local church. Some have literally interviewed other organizations to find a better match for their spiritual needs. Is it too much to ask, if a religion is preaching intolerance of others and preaching pernicious superstition and outdated philosophy over rational reasoning, that the members should look for a more loving, tolerant faith?

The vast majority of believers today are good people. They get comfort and satisfaction from believing in a god and from practicing their faith by participating in the social group of a church community. With the literally thousands of varieties of religion available, some must practice a faith based on a loving and compassionate god who does not require believers to use a holy book that is filled with hate, jealousy and anger. With two new religions being formed every day, perhaps it is already there; if not, why not start one?

What are the good parts of most religions and which parts need to be discarded?

There are many good parts of most major religions, including those features which reward positive, loving behavior toward other people. The comfort the faithful get from prayer seems to provide value to members of many faiths. Worshipping together in a social setting and all the other social benefits of being with like-minded people all seem very positive. There are many excellent, valuable programs of assistance for the disadvantaged and support for the victims of life's hardships that organized religion now provides support.

First in the "must-go" column is the concept of immutability, of being fixed and not changing. Everything does change, we learn new things all the time, and any faith that is fixed as to its scripture is doomed to be left behind. That does not mean it cannot have a human moral code that is commendable and to even take the high ground of rewarding what is morally right. I know that most religions have an "immutability clause" dominating their lists of beliefs, but this is a core problem; life just does not work that way. Society, culture, and our way of life changes; religion has to be adaptable to continue to be useful to its followers. I don't mean constantly changing with every whim. A religious system can be designed to be difficult to change; many important things in a society are made difficult to change in order to make sure change is truly warranted. Our Constitution comes to mind. We have the ability to make revisions in the document, but they are hard to implement, as they should be; nevertheless, change is not impossible. As good as we all think the Constitution is, we recognize that a method of change is necessary.

Second, the jealousy and sanctioned violence by god has to go. I know violence is culturally variable and is even considered desirable in some circumstances. Protection of our families and our property is often seen as a justifiable reason for violence. I certainly agree; I know I could become very violent if my family were threatened. But let's keep such action in the domain of civil law and advance religion into the positive side of human interaction. As human animals, we should all be fully aware of what we are capable of doing to each other. When it comes to violence against our own species, we are likely the most vicious and violent of all animals. We don't need scriptures to encourage us to carry out that violence on other people. A focus on love and understanding, rather than hatred and killing, is what I'm suggesting here.

Third, jealousy on the part of the deity of one's faith has to go. Jealousy as a trait of a monotheistic god seems to be an oxymoron. After all, if the god is the one and only, who does it have to be jealous of? The tremendous, violently expressed anxiety of followers of Islam in response to any perceived "dissing" of their god is amazing. Remember the world-wide reaction to the Mohammed cartoons published in a Danish newspaper? Maybe I'm missing something, but omnipotent pretty much says it all, and all the rules about not taking any other gods, and commandments about keeping this god supreme, seem a little silly if he/it is the omnipotent one-and-only. Therefore, all the jealousy being taught in scriptures needs to go. Despite what is said in the scriptures, being jealous is not a positive attribute for a god or a believer.

Next, the creation story has to go, or at least it has to allow for what science and common sense dictates as the truth about the evolution of life on earth. Evolving understanding of nature is important and needs to be added to the positive side of things religious; we need to accept and support continued research and development of scientific knowledge; the constant conflict between science and religion needs to end. There must be a way of conceptualizing things so that those who wish to believe can allow that their god can take responsibility for what happens after death, and meanwhile let science get on with making the world a better and more understood place to live while we are alive on this earth.

The expectation that a prophet is going to return, and that this world as we know it is going to be destroyed, must also go. This is a common theme in many religions, expounded by many prophets. It stops otherwise rational people from having the motivation to take care of this planet. Our environment is at risk, and thinking that it does not matter because the end is near does not help. James Watt, the Secretary of the Interior under Ronald Reagan, said, *"We don't have to protect the environment. The Second Coming is at hand."* This attitude, that we as humans are so special, that the earth was created for us to use, and it just does not matter because it is all just temporary anyway, is self-destructive, to be sure. This is no legacy to leave to our children and grandchildren who will inherit what we have neglected.

In summary, the things to look for in a new faith are the comfort it can provide to believers in prayer and the humanitarian assistance it can provide for the disadvantaged, as well as the positive social participation, equality between the sexes, tolerance for differences, and love and understanding for all. The short list of what has to go includes the immutability of scripture and the violence and the jealousy of its gods, as well as religion's hostility to scientific advancement and knowledge. For those who wish to find such a modern faith and enjoy the benefits of believing, there are probably many choices.

Fourth, we can work toward modernization of the major monotheistic faiths. Perhaps Bishop Spong is correct in feeling that, once people in the Christian faith realize that their choice is modernization or extinction, they will update their scriptures, keep the good parts, and renounce the hate. I'm far less optimistic than he is about this, but I do think we can make a start by educating our children about the history and foundations of the major faiths. The goal is not to keep them from believing in their parents' faith, but rather to encourage independent thinking that will encourage modernizing steps that will bring these religions into alignment with the necessary features of a peaceful world. As an educator, I have hope that the youth of our world will take the steps necessary to live in peace, once they understand the shortcomings as well as advantages of the current monotheistic beliefs and that living with religious tolerance is an option. We have seen many religious revolutions evolve out of the original "children of Abraham;" perhaps it is not too much to hope for a religion to evolve, before it is too late, based on love of diversity.

We can also ask our friends who belong to traditional, monotheistic religions how they see their faith evolving into a more tolerant religion. We expect our technology to keep moving forward, and we expect our health care to be up to date; why can't we expect our religions to fit the age we live in? Let's face it -- the Internet was not around two thousand years ago, and Facebook and Twitter were not how people communicated, but they are now. We have learned that we all descended from the same humanoids barely walking upright on their way out of Africa. We know now that the earth is approximately 4.5 billion years old, and life has existed on this planet for millions of years. And, yes, we don't know everything, but we admit it and keep learning. We need a god that will help us learn to live together as one species that will help us take care of the only planet we have. The scriptures of two thousand years ago do not do that. Either get a new book or get a new god with a new book that allows for new editions.

Fifth, my last suggestion for a solution to these problems of the monotheistic faiths is for growth of and acceptance of rational, moral non-belief. A secular society based upon logic, rational thought, and evidence-based scientific reasoning is another option. I do not think nonbelievers are missing out on anything. We can be just as awe-struck about beauty, art, music, love of one another and just as happy, which is likely the goal we all seek. In fact, western religion does not correlate very well with happiness. A University of California San Francisco Medical Center study, using brain scans of Buddhist test subjects, showed they were likely to be happier and calmer than most other people. Another study of over eighty thousand people from all countries in the world was used to create the "World Map of Happiness." This study found that happiness does not correlate very well with highly religious, compared to less religious people. In fact, nine of the ten happiest countries are listed in the top twenty-eight predominantly secular countries in the world. The United States is not one of the top ten happy countries, but Canada is number ten in happiness (yet, number 20 as predominantly nonreligious) and Sweden is number 7th in happiness and is also the most nonreligious country in the world. I know that many individuals who pray to their god feel happiness as a result and genuinely feel good about their faith. Yet, I want to point out that, when whole cultures are reviewed, nonbelievers can be just as happy.

What would happen to a society if it became less religious? Well let's look at the least religious countries in the world and see if they have fallen apart? Phil Zuckerman has done what is likely to be the most comprehensive analysis of such countries. The 2004 United Nations' Human Development Report ranked 177 countries on a human development index and found that the top five nations were Norway, Sweden, Australia, Canada and the Netherlands. Zuckerman says these are among the most stable, peaceful, free, wealthy, healthy societies, and they contain the highest percentage of atheists and agnostics. For example, between 46 and 85 percent of Sweden's population are nonbelievers. Now it would be a problem to automatically associate this correlation as signifying cause, based on just these two items, but it does support the argument that becoming less religious would not result in cultural disaster.

If, as a society, we stopped believing all the negative, harmful scriptures, and maybe even gave up the angry, jealous god, would we also have to give up all the good parts of religion? I don't know why this should be the case. There is a lot to like about religion that can be retained -- the friendships, the dinners, and the music. We could even keep attending weekly meetings where a wise, loving leader could suggest ways to improve ourselves and our relationships with those who are different and yet so interesting. I certainly would not give up my Christmas music, my holiday tree, and all the wonderful traditions my family enjoys. The bottom line is that being free of faith is nothing to fear.

Nonbelievers are only different in that they do not spend time in prayer, they don't avoid analytical science, and they don't put much effort into trying to figure out the confusing messages in a 1600 year-old book. Freeing all people to think rationally about any subject and to appreciate the science of the cosmos, as well as the interdependence of all life on this planet, would be a giant step forward for humanity.

The good that is done by religions can be done by secular organizations, including social clubs and other charitable groups. No one would argue that religious groups do not do a lot of good and help a lot of needy people. On the other hand, I'm not so sure that good is always done by the proselytizing objectives of the missionaries of monotheistic faiths. Consider this, as stated by Jomo Kenyatta, the first prime minister and president of independent Kenya: *"When the missionaries arrived, the Africans had the land and the missionaries had the Bible. They taught us how to pray with our eyes closed. When we opened them, they had the land and we had the Bible."* From my point of view, it is difficult to see why a religion needs to proselytize itself to people who already have a religious belief. If people are happy with their faith, why would you want to convert them? But then, from my point of view, it is not the belief in a god that is the problem; it is the scriptures that teach the hatred and intolerance. Therefore, believing in any one god or gods is about the same as believing in any other to me.

Morality, or the lack of it, is always mentioned when discussing the possibility of non-religion. There are good believers and there are bad believers; the same is true for discredists. With hundreds of major religions all having rules to live by, fixed values that are generally similar on the major points, one gets the idea that people have about the same moral codes everywhere. How can any one religion think that it provides the only correct moral foundation?

It has been intriguing to learn about many of the values expressed in the eastern religions. For the most part, I have been very impressed with how loving and caring the followers of these faiths are toward their fellow humans. I suspect that, without the hatred fueled by western scriptures, we might be able to solve many of the problems of world health, reduce the needlessly high death rates of children, and allow our scientists to do the research needed to reduce unnecessary suffering. As mentioned previously, we do not need commandments from an invisible god to do the right thing. Nonbelievers are just as moral as believers; without the foundational intolerances found in western scriptures which hinder morality, we could even be better.

We don't have to stop dreaming in an evolved, secular world. We can examine the most incredible complexities of our universe and look for evidence of our wildest dreams. We can be "spiritual," moved with awe at the wonders of this magnificent planet and what is beyond. Most of all, we can be moved by the complexity and wonder of the human animal, its beauty, and its capacity to love, if given a chance -- if not taught to hate. A world full of rational, caring people who strive to live in balance with our planet, to help all humankind live a better, happier life without religious books filled with hate and violence or any jealous war gods, is a future world worth striving for.

It should be obvious by this point that I think religion and the belief in a supernatural deity are built into most humans, and this proclivity is so strong that the possibility of rapidly moving to a secular world community is low. However, it could happen, and I think it eventually will, if this world doesn't end in some nuclear fireball called "Revelation." The human species evolves pretty fast, socially and culturally, when things become uncomfortable; so maybe it will happen, at least in time for my grandchildren.

Here are my bottom-line prescriptions for a better world:

First, talk, listen, and think about the unreasonableness of half of the world's people believing in scripture written thousands of years ago in a violent, ignorant time, in a very desperately difficult part of the world. Realize the folly of making those writings the inerrant guideline of how we should live now. If possible, take an objective look at these books, think about what they say, and ask yourself if these are suitable guides as to how we should live and think today.

Second, support separation of church and state and encourage everyone to remove religion from community activities. If prayer and religious acts are not the forum for and not the purpose of the event, it has no place at the event. We have a lot to be proud of in America. The freedom to practice any belief is one; the clear, legally binding law to separate church and state is another one.

Third, learn all you can about all the religions and how they impact this planet and the people on it. Encourage others to learn about their own religion, its history and its likely future. Being educated is being able to apply knowledge and information in rational and logical ways. Work towards educating our youth in all aspects of religion as an objective subject, not as faith. There is plenty of time for young people to make their own decisions on what they want to believe.

Fourth, question everything. Ask for evidence for what is said to be true; ask for reasons for why people do what they do. Science and the scientific method of learning have proven to work. No one wants to return to the dark ages. If it sounds like magic or superstition, then ask about it. Encourage our media and our political leaders to see and talk clearly about religion so that, when it is the story behind the news, this aspect is honestly and accurately reported. We are long past the point where it is appropriate to be politically "polite," to ignore violence, abuse, and ignorance in the name of religion.

And finally, be tolerant and kind. Make the effort to understand how others think, their points of view, and, if they believe in a religion, find out what they believe and why. Remember, there is no scientific evidence that a god exists, but there is also no evidence that one, or many, do not exist. A belief requires no evidence. In fact, a belief is what people want to be true, and, who knows? It might just be true, even though not "provable." By acting in a loving, moral, open-minded and compassionate manner, we can all make this world a better place to live and thus, a better place for our children and grandchildren. It is time!

Bibliography

Ali, Ayaan Hirs. 2007. *Infidel.* New York: Free Press

Armstrong, Karen. 1993. *A History of God The 4,000 Year Quest of Judaism, Christianity and Islam.* New York: Balentine Books.

Atran, Scott. 2002. *In Gods We Trust: The Evolutionary Landscape of Religion.* New York. Oxford University Press

Barker, Dan. 2008. *Godless, How an Evangelical Preacher Became One of America's Leading Atheists.* Berkeley, California. ULYSSES PRESS

Besant, Annie. 1915. *The Basis of Morality.* Madras, India. Theosophical Publishing House.

Boyer, Pascal. 2001. *Religion Explained: The evolutionary Origins of Religious Thought.* New York: Perseus Books Group

Buckman, Robert. 2002. *Can We Be Good Without God? Biology, Behavior, and the Need to Believe.* Amherst, New York: Prometheus Books

Carrier, Richard. 2005. *Sense & Goodness Without God a Defense of Metaphysical Naturalism.* Bloominton, Indiana: AuthorHouse

Darwish, Nonie. 2008. *Cruel and Usual Punishment.* Thomas Nelson, Nashville Tennessee

Dawkins, Richard. 1996. *The Blind Watchmaker.* New York: W W Norton And Company

Dawkins, Richard. 2008. *The God Delusion.* New York: A Mariner Book Houghton Mifflin Company

Dennett, Daniel C. 2006. *Breaking The Spell Religion as a Natural Phenomenon.* New York: Penquin Group.

Dennett, Daniel C. 1995. *Darwin's Dangerous Idea: Evolution and Meanings of Life.* New York: Simon & Schuster Paperbacks

Diamond, Jared. 2006. *The Third chimpanzee: The evolution and Future of the Human Animal.* New York: W.W. Norton & Co.

Diamond, Jared. 2005. *Guns, Germs, and Steel: The Fates of Human Societies.* New York: W.W. Norton & Co.

Draper, John William. *History of the Conflict between Religion and Science.* Ebook transfer.

Edis, Taner. 2008. *Science and Nonbelief.* Amherst, New York: Prometheus Books

Ellerbe, Helen. 1995. *The Dark Side of Christian History.* San Rafael, CA: Morningstar Books

Eller, David. 2007. *Atheism Advanced*. Cranford, New Jersey: American Atheist Press.

Eller, David. 2004. *Natural Atheism*. Cranford, New Jersey: American Atheist Press.

Gould, Stephen Jay. 1990. *Wonderful Life The burgess Shale and the Nature of History*. New York: W. W. Norton & Company.

Gibbons, David. 2007. *Faiths and Religions Of The World*. *San Diego*, California: Thunder Bay Press.

Guillaume, Alfred. 1986. *Islam*. England: Penguin Books.

Harris, Sam. 2004. *The End of Faith: Religion, Terror, and the Future of Reason*. London, England: W.W. Norton & Company Ltd.

Harris, Sam. 2008. *Letter to a Christian Nation*. New York: Vintage Books

Hawking, Stephen. 2005. *A Briefer History of Time*. New York: Bantam Dell

Hawking, Stephen. 2001. *The Universe in a Nutshell*. New York: Bantam Books

Hedges Chris, 2006. *American Fascists – The Christian Right and the War on America*. New York, NY. Free Press Simon & Schuster, Inc.

Hitchens, Christopher. 2007. *God is Not Great.* New York: Hachette Book Group USA

Hitchens, Christopher. 2007. *The Portable Atheist.* Philadelphia, PA: Perseus Books

Huberman, Jack. 2007. *The quotable Atheist*, New York: Nation Books.

Keene, Michael. 2002. *World Religions.* London, England: Westminster John Knox Press

Kirsch, Jonathan. 2004. *God Against The Gods: The History of the War Between Monotheism and Polytheism.* London, England: Pequin Books

Lama, Dalai. 1999. *Spiritual Advice For Buddhists and Christians.* New York: Continuum Publishing

Lippmann, Walter. 1957. *A Preface To Morals.* New York: Time Reading Program

Mortenson, Greg.- Relin, David Oliver. 2006. *Three Cups of Tea,* New York: Penguin Books

Miller, Kenneth R. 1999. *Finding Darwin's God.* New York: Harper Perennial

Nairn, Rob. 2004. *Living Dreaming Dying: Practical Wisdom from the Tibetan Book of the Dead.* Boston, MA: Shambhala

Nicholson, Reynold A. 1989. *The Mystics of Islam.* England: Penguin Books.

Ray, Darrel W. 2009. *The God Virus: How Religion Infects Our Lives and Culture.* Bonner Springs, Kansas: IPC Press

Raymo, Chet. 1998. Skeptics And True Believers: The Exhilarating Connection Between Science and Religion. New York: MJF Books

Russell, Bertrand. 1957. Why I Am Not a Christian. New York: A Touchstone Book

Steele, David Ramsy. 2008. *Atheism Explained from Folly to Philosophy.* Chicago, Illinois: Open Court.

Schaeffer, Frank. 2007. *Crazy for God.* Cambridge, MA: DA Capo Press

Smith, Huston. 1991. *The World's Religions – Our Great Wisdom Traditions.* San Francisco, CA: HarperSanFrancisco

Spence, Lewis. 2004. *Myths Legends of the North American Indians.* London, England: CRW Publishing Limited

Spong, John Shelby. 2005. *The Sins of Scripture.* San Francisco, CA: HarperSanFracisco

Spong, John Shelby. 2007. *Jesus for the Non-Religious: Recovering the Divine at the Heart of the Human.* San Francisco, CA: HarperSanFracisco

St Rain, Justice. 2003. *My Baha'i Faith.* Heltonville, IN: National Spiritual Assembly of the United States

The Book of Mormon. 1948. Salt Lake City, Utah: The Church of Jesus Christ of Latter-day Saints

The Bible. Revised Standard Version. 1973. New York: American Bible Society.

The Qur'an. Translated by M.H. Shakir. 1997. New York: Tahrike Tarsile Qur'an, Inc.

White, Gayle Colquitt. 1997. *Believers and Beliefs – A Practical Guide to Religious Etiquette for Business and Social Occasions.* New York: Berkley Book

Wilson, Edward O. 2004. (orig. 1978) *On Human Nature.* Harvard University Press, London, England.

Index

7910 N Denver
Portland, OR 97217